ANCIENT EMPIRES OF THE NEW AGE

ANCIENT EMPIRES
OF THE
NEW AGE

*Paul deParrie
and
Mary Pride*

CROSSWAY BOOKS • WESTCHESTER, ILLINOIS
A DIVISION OF GOOD NEWS PUBLISHERS

Ancient Empires of the New Age.

Copyright © 1989 by Paul deParrie and Mary Pride.

Published by Crossway Books, a division of
Good News Publishers, Westchester, Illinois 60154.

Cover Image: Michel Tcherevkoff / The Image Bank

Second printing, 1989

Printed in the United States of America

Library of Congress Catalog Card Number 89-50335

ISBN 0-89107-530-5

Bible verses are quoted from *Holy Bible: New International Version*,
copyright © 1978 by the New York International Bible Society.
Used by permission of Zondervan Bible Publishers.

CONTENTS

INTRODUCTION

What You Always Wanted to Know About the New Age, But Were Too Confused to Ask

I t's lunchtime, but you're not hungry yet. And, since you're at the mall, what could be more natural than killing some time at the bookstore?

So in you wander, lugging a half-filled shopping bag, hoping the store detective won't mistake you for a shoplifter. You stroll past the Sports section (lots of baseball bios this year), the Humor section (oh, good, there's that hot new book you've been meaning to get), turn a corner, and there it is.

The New Age section!

A year or two ago there was no such thing as a New Age zone in your average local bookstore. Not even at the mall. A whole double-sided rack devoted to New Age books seemed a fainter prospect than a presidential victory for the Democratic party.

Now this long-unnoticed literary void has been filled. But with what? You pass quickly over the tomes on UFO's, crystals, channeling, and astrology. That's all old hat by now — only the *National Enquirer* is still fascinated by these subjects. Pyramid power? Dream interpretations? Same old stuff (no wonder it's not selling!).

Ah, but here on the next shelf! Take a look at *this!*

Practical Egyptian Magic.[1] *Practical Celtic Magic.*[2] *Secret Native American Pathways.*[3] *The Mayan Factor.*[4] . . .

"Hey, wait a minute! I thought this was the *New* Age section. What's with all these ancient Egyptians, Druids, Mayans, and whatnot?"

We're so glad you asked!

We're not the first people to point out that the "New" Age is not exactly new.[5] The more you look into it, the more it resembles an all-you-can-eat spiritual smorgasbord: a dash of Egyptian *kusherie* here, some Greek *moussaka* there, a heaping helping of Aztec amaranth crackers and some Babylonian fortune cookies, all toasted lightly in the smoke from a Native American peace pipe and delivered to your door by the friendly little green guy in the flying saucer. It's like one of those old movies you see on the "Late-Late Show": *Abbot and Costello Meet the Mummy, Nimrod, Zeus, Dagon, Dracula, the Wolfman, Godzilla, and E.T.* It's like someone took all of ancient history, mixed in a hundred issues of *Amazing Stories*, stuffed it into a great big bag, twirled it over his head three times, and turned it loose in Dubuque, Iowa.

So here you have the goddess Diana from Greece rubbing shoulders with Isis from Egypt. Over there a dedicated little band is trying to revive nature worship; over here some true believers claim they are descendants of starship travelers. Here a Mayan, there an Aztec, everywhere a feathered shaman. On top of all this, you find the scientific types trying to drag every New Age belief into the mainstream by relabeling, say, spirit-possession during séances as "archetypes of the collective unconscious"[6] or exaggerating the piezoelectric qualities of the crystals that less-enlightened New Agers wear as amulets.[7]

Not only that, but a concerted attempt is now being made in public schools, public TV, pool halls, and other highly intellectual platforms to discredit Christianity as a series of "myths." You know, like Santa Claus and the Tooth Fairy. Meanwhile, the very same school kids who aren't allowed to hear a breath of Bible teaching during, before, or after school hours are being taught that witchcraft is a *serious religion* that deserves our respect and not just a silly superstition patronized by weird ladies in funny hats.

It is fair to say that, in spite of *Star Trek* and *She-Ra*, America was not prepared for this. Although the Supreme Court may have decided to ban all traces of Christianity from the public schools and anywhere else someone might be affected by it, there still is a gut feeling in the hills of Tennessee that this is a Christian nation. But to go to the mall and see all that gosh-awful *heathen* stuff — well, Pa, what is this world coming to?

We don't blame you for being confused. Religion today is like trying to eat dinner in a restaurant with a huge menu in a foreign language. You had enough trouble sorting out the Methodists, Charismatics, Presbyterians, and Catholics, and now you have to worry about the Church of Wicca and the Temple of the Golden Dawn, not to mention your assorted Hare Krishnas, Baal-worshipers, Hermetics, Rosicrucians, nature cults, Pan-cults, Isis-lovers, Mithraists, Druids, and so on.

If, as some claim, all religions are the same and all lead in the same direction, how come we need so many *new* ones? And why is it that the new ones don't resemble the old ones at all?

We are here to help you translate the menu and sort out the clutter. The New Age in all its bewildering apparent diversity didn't come out of nowhere, or even out of the thirteenth chapter of the book of Revelation. It has a past, quite a long one, in fact, as we will show. It is by no means the dynamic young infant its promoters make it out to be. Nor is the New Age inevitably successful; as we will show, it has declined and fallen as often as it has arisen. Nor is this the first appearance of the New Age in the Western world; as we will also show, such outbreaks have occurred with monotonous consistency ever since the Christian missionaries converted Europe. Since we're sure you're curious, we will also look at *why* and *how* the New Age arose and faded each time . . . and why it is doomed to fade out yet again.

We like to write about success, but this is a book about failure. Not only is the New Age not new, it has been a failure every time any culture has adopted it. We are going to peek behind the gold-coating on the New Age image and discover its feet of clay. We are going to discover why there is *no* reason for Christians to assume that this precise period of human history is The End, and what steps Christians can take to keep it from happening.

We are not prejudiced against the New Age. To be prejudiced means to judge something without seeing it . . . and we've seen plenty. One of us is a converted occultist, and the other a converted humanist. Between us, we have experienced the two wings of the New Age and can testify that the bird can't fly.

So come travel with us to the *real* sources of the New Age. Tour the Hanging Gardens of Babylon and the Rambo architecture of Sargon's palace in Assyria. Meet Osiris, the Wimp of the Gods, and watch the Greek and Roman gods disappear before your very eyes. Discover why the Hindus and Buddhists want to *escape* reincarnation; why Aztec temples do not belong on packages of health-food crackers; and why Babylon got turned into a dust bowl. Follow the wavering course of our very own Western pagan movements, from the Montanists of the 160s to the Theosophists of the 1860s, and find out why the New Age is actually about three hundred years behind schedule. Find out what fatal error on the part of the Christian church finally changed the climate of the Western world so that the dragons were emboldened to return, and how the church has dealt with these ancient dragons before.

Old, frowsty dragons . . .

Dragons covered with cobwebs . . .

Dragons with long, white beards . . .

PART 1

THE NOT-SO-NEW AGE

CHAPTER 1

A QUICKIE FIELD GUIDE TO THE NEW AGE

When men tell you to consult mediums and spiritists, who whisper and mutter, should not a people inquire of their God? Why consult the dead on behalf of the living? To the law and to the testimony! If they do not speak according to this word, they have no light of dawn.

—Isaiah 8:19, 20

What do you think of when you hear the word "pagan"? Stolid idols surrounded by offerings of flowers and incense? Capering witch doctors? Seventeenth-century cannibals warming up the pot for the local missionary?

These all are true pictures of paganism in its pre-Madison Avenue stage. But paganism is not limited to primitive societies. It can flourish in the presence of toaster ovens and central heating — although we admit pagan societies of the past have done little to invent such devices.

We are going to prove in this book that the so-called New Age is nothing but toaster oven paganism. It is nothing more or less than a conglomeration of the worn-out pagan doctrines of failed ancient empires.

For the benefit of those readers who are not yet well-acquainted with New Age teaching, we will begin with a brief recap of a few favorite New Age beliefs, so you will be sure to recognize them when we tour ancient Babylon and the other pagan empires.

Roll-Your-Own Religion

Western — and particularly American — paganism preaches that each person must "do what is right *for him*." Thus people tend to select bits and pieces of various practices and glom them together as the fancy suits them. This is the way popular religion, as opposed to the official religion, has been practiced in most ancient cultures.

New Agers in general are not exclusively loyal to any one type of teaching or practice. Also, most pagan practices fit into several different categories at once. For instance, much of what a shaman does falls under spiritism; sympathetic magic is tied closely with animism. In New Age religion, you roll your own.

Divination

Astrology, the teaching that the stars in the sky guide our lives, is the most popular form of divination in the West. It is the gateway by which many enter the pagan religion. Like all other techniques for predicting the future, astrology puts Nature in control and dispenses with the sovereignty of God.

Divination is completely amoral. The stars never guide you to make *righteous* choices, or even hint that righteousness exists. The pervert and the upright all receive their readings on an equal basis.

The Bible prohibits astrology, absolutely and completely. In fact, part of the reason for God's judgment of Babel was the tower built "unto the heavens."

In ancient times, the future was divined by sheep livers and chicken entrails. The Babylonians devoted thousands of volumes to the "science" of liver divination. To them, these copious observations constituted the pinnacle of science. The number of followers of these practices today — at least in the West — is negligible. Tea-leaf diviners and palm readers, once so popular, are also now on the wane. Instead, the curious and the serious both seem to favor Tarot cards and I Ching.

Spiritism

While séances are not as popular as they once were, channeling has taken the Western world by storm. The dark rooms, trumpets, floating tables, ectoplasm, and dead Uncle

Harry's voice have been replaced by bright lights and "voices" which speak in Near East accents with a dash of King James English.

Today, one of the most-used forms of spiritism is contact with a "spirit guide." You empty your mind and bingo! something is speaking to you, or even appearing before you. (This is quite different from Christian prayer, where your mind stays active and focused on God's Word.)

An interesting question is what exactly those spirit guides are. Christians, of course, recognize so-called spirit guides as old-fashioned demons, and the process of emptying one's mind to receive one as an invitation to demon possession. Demon possession, however, does not sell, so the demons are being billed as wonderful helpers who will lead you to godhood as long as you are willing to totally surrender to their leadership.

Mystic New Agers see their guides as one of the gods, an angel, a dead person, or an ascended master like Buddha. A humanist will see it as himself talking to himself — a hidden part of his own mind. Under the pretense that spirit guides are simply "imaginary friends," public school teachers in some schools are leading little children to invite such guides into their lives.

Most adult New Age types view the guide as "the God within." For some this allows them to skip the gurus and swamis and go directly to the Source (the demons) and become "self-guided." One writer explains:

> I know this sounds far-fetched, part of the faddish trend toward self-actualization workshops, psychics, channels and spirit mediums like Ramtha, Seth (and Boopsie's "Hunk-Ra" in Doonesbury). All these things can be expensive and addictive. But the guide meditation is free and done in solitude, making me dependent on no one but myself and solely responsible for my own "movie," as the jargon has it. The phrase "we create our own reality" is demonstrated by me to me through this meditation.[1]

The Bible prohibits seeking contact with spirits other than God — be they billed as dead people, demons, ascended masters, spirit guides, or aliens. These contacts, whether made by Ouija boards, automatic writing, channeling, meditation, or centering, are *all* dangerous.

New Agers fail to take into account that they have no way to check the accuracy of the spirits' claims. Generally they assume the spirit is a "good spirit." In fact, very many New Agers assume *all* spirits are good. The Bible, on the other hand, flatly states that all such contacts are evil.

Channeled spirits seem to have very little imagination. Over and over they offer the same basic teachings. The first is, "Thou art God." This familiar lie, dating back to the Garden of Eden, is then linked with the teaching that "all you need for salvation (enlightenment, or whatever) is within you." Oddly enough, the ground rules then state that you have to totally surrender to the control of the spirit in order to experience this wonderful godhood and freedom. All you need to become free is to make yourself the spirit's slave.

Shamanism

A shaman is a person who serves as a spiritual leader because of his alleged ability to contact and control spiritual forces, often with the use of "power animals" or totems (e.g., your basic black cat). This, by the way, is also the textbook definition of a sorcerer, but "shaman" still sounds better than "sorcerer" to the man in the street.[2]

The visual image of the shaman is that of a witch doctor with feathered headdress and bone ornaments. While this type of shaman is beginning to return in the West, most modern shamans skip the feathers.

Like the channeled entities (and, as we will see, like certain popular psychologists), shamans often refer the seeker to his own inner guidance as the way to truth. Acting on impulse in this manner, just like you did when you were a baby crying in dirty diapers, is called "intuitive" by New Age pagans. They make much of the difference between the freedom of intuitive living as opposed to the strictures of "living by rigid rules" (although, oddly enough, no New Ager so far has come out against toilet training).

The shaman himself attempts his cures and other spiritual processes by "intuitive" ceremonies and spells.

America, staggering under the burden of centuries of medical advancements, now suffers from a woeful lack of these talented people. So classes are offered in most major American cities in shamanistic dancing and drumming, the making of medicine bags, peyote beading, and power animal contacts. Coming soon to a state university near you.

Animism

Here is your good old-fashioned all-African paganism with which we are so familiar. Animism is the belief that spirits or powers inhabit objects and "animate" them. Pantheism, the belief that all nature is God, falls under this category, as does the belief that individual spirit beings inhabit the trees, rocks, wind, etc. A deeper look at most of these teachings reveals a belief in *mana*, a nameless, faceless power, not dissimilar to "The Force" as portrayed in the movie *Star Wars*.

The use of amulets, talismans, crystals, or symbols to bring power, luck, or "energies" to bear is an extension of this belief. This, of course, is unbiblical and denies the sovereignty of God. If powers reside in objects to be used at will by any individual, then God is unnecessary.

Mystery Religions

Mystery religions do not necessarily focus on a particular god or goddess, but they do thrive on claims that they hold secret knowledge that leads to God, happiness, Nirvana, or whatever.

Most of these cults appeal to the "wisdom of the ancients." Rosicrucians claim to possess the wisdom of Egypt and Babylon. Mainline New Agers are fond of asserting *they* have the good word from Atlantis (a neat trick since they have not even found Atlantis yet). Mormons vigorously maintain that they, and they alone, have the records of otherwise unknown ancient American civilizations.

Secret initiation rites and special knowledge are the earmarks of these cults. Often Christianity is accused of being just another of the mystery religions that sprang up around the time of Christ. Those who say this, claim that baptism and communion were the initiation rites. But there is nothing *hidden* about baptism or communion — in fact, outsiders are *urged* to attend Christian worship.

The Apostle Paul speaks eloquently about the "mysteries of the faith," but only in the context of their being *revealed* mysteries. Most of this mystery, Paul claims, was hidden until Christ. Unlike the mystery cults, though, the mysteries were even hidden from the prophets who proclaimed them — hidden from the chief initiates.

The mystery cults are designed to *exclude* people from God, happiness, Nirvana, or whatever, unless they qualify in intelligence, wisdom, or some other ability. Jesus Christ was sent to *include* people.

Idolatry

When people think of paganism, they usually think first of idolatry. They picture wood or stone figures surrounded by dancing and bowing people; a fat, smiling Buddha with clouds of incense rising before him; or the superheated arms of a brass Molech awaiting the tiny, squirming infant sacrifice.

But idolatry, by God's definition, is when *anything* is placed ahead of Him. For this reason Scripture condemns covetousness as idolatry. Career, wealth, convenience, possessions, and popularity can all fill the bill, but the common element of them all is *self*. In all of these — and many others — man vaunts *his will* before God.

The most common idol worshiped in the West today lives in the mirror. Even the atheist does his homage at the silvered glass altar. As my (Paul's) son observed when he was three years old, "People that say there is no God — it's because they think that *they* are God." I think both Scripture and experience will bear out this simple truth.

Now being layered over this cultural selfishness is the "Thou art God" teaching of the New Age pagans.

"To find God," intones one master, "Be yourself."[3]

Another says, "I've found humility in acknowledging the power I have in creating all that comes to me. The being and doing of my life, as wretched and wonderful as it is, is the perfect unfolding of me."[4] (Lord, preserve us from such "humility.")

Have you fallen down and worshiped New Ager Chris Pringer today? He thinks you should. This man says, "My part of the Plan for Earth is being restored. I Am That I Am, (through me) the Power of All Life manifested."[5]

Enough, already! We're sure you get the idea.

This is not to say that traditional idolatry is not being practiced today in the West. Far from it. Many writers and speakers now recommend resurrecting the ancient pantheons and especially the worship of the Mother Goddess. But so far it's easier to tease people into mooning into their mirrors than into investing in bulky statues that clutter up their living rooms.

Sympathetic Magic

Sympathetic magic, often called Earth magic, claims that natural laws as seen in the visible sphere affect the spiritual realm as well. For instance, since dirt brings about growth in seeds, then dirt might be selected for any spell or medicine bag related to growth. So if you want to grow tall like Dr. J., eat some dirt, or roll in the dirt, or rub dirt in your hair. For *real* power, use the dirt off a tall basketball player's sneakers. Yum! It is a practice associated with shamanism.

> The Law of Similarity: This is the basis of all "sympathetic magick" (ex. voodoo dolls) [sic]. Actions done to an object also effect the object or entity which is like it. The ASSO-CIATION may only exist in the mind of the magician.[6]

Unhappily, the more hard-core New Agers have discovered that in ancient occult thinking *blood* is the most powerful substance you can use.

> Blood has the most potent vibration of any substance on the planet, and is used in most magic work. Tibetan lamas still use it today. It is well known that when you release blood from your body you get power; many men who were in Viet-nam can attest to this magical potency of the spilling of "the dark forces." The planet needs blood to be released, it needs it in some way to feed the planet [the Goddess, Mother Earth?] and maintain natural balance. [7]

Interesting ecology, this. Our planet wants blood. It's a big planet and must have a big appetite. Releasing blood from *your* body (we're not talking chicken blood here) gives power. Human blood=power. Mother Earth wants to eat *you*.

Watch out where this blood-thirsty trend leads. It could get nasty.

Hinduism

We have a whole chapter on Hinduism later, but we need to mention it quickly here because the two most basic New Age doctrines are reincarnation (the notion that you will be reborn into many future lives) and karma (the notion that the good and the ill in your present life comes as a direct result of your actions in a previous life). These two doctrines are at the roots of a whole series of abuses.

The cycle of reincarnation and karma presupposes a "works" salvation, and an unlimited number of tries for the goal. Unfortunately, the goal is not worth having, since Hindu heaven is to *escape* the cycle of reincarnation and become gobbled up into the god Brahmin, avoiding the endless misery of suffering and dying in life after life. Westerners, with their Christian ideas, have not yet realized that reincarnation is not really a cute way to avoid the doctrine of Hell — it *is* Hell.

This life isn't the greatest either, since everything bad that happens to you is *your own fault* and deserves no sympathy from others. If you're poor and sick, man, you done it to yourself. On the other hand, if you are rich and healthy, you have no obligation to spread the blessing around. Any suffering you inflict on your social inferiors is their own fault for having bad karma. Such is the compassionate New Age teaching.

Syncretism

Syncretism is the attempt to blend many religions into an amorphous mass. It's the teaching that, since all roads lead t) God, you might as well buy a EuroRail pass and try them all out.

During the Roman Empire the mystery religions, philosophers, gnostics, and others all tried to absorb Christianity into their happy little syncretism — but without success.

Pagans today try to imply that Biblical Judaism and Christianity are actually syncretistic religions. They point to similarities between Creation and Flood legends of Babylon and the Biblical accounts, then imply that the Biblical accounts were borrowed from the pagan nations. But a close investigation shows that it happened the other way around. The pagan versions are distorted, with their totally impossible adventures of emotional gods and mythical beasts, in contrast to the restrained sensibleness of the Biblical accounts.

Syncretism demands *tolerance* of differences in pagan teachings. This is accomplished by the teaching that each person has *his own path*. Even when New Age publications carry articles based on opposing premises, it makes little difference since all paths lead to the same place.

Today's Western pagans can simply select anything from a smorgasbord of religious ideas and concoct their own private religion. They can even toss out old pieces and add new ones with abandon and it is viewed as part of their own evolution — their own path. The only way you can come up with anything these people will look upon with contempt is if you claim to know the One Right Way. (It's OK to know the One Best Way, as long as it's only best for *you*.) Once you claim to know the One Right Way, the gloves come off. You will be labeled unenlightened,[8] a fundamentalist fascist,[9] ignorant,[10] a dark pocket of resistance,[11] an idolater,[12] negative,[13] inferior,[14] unfit,[15] and "antichrist."[16] All in the name of universal love and peace and brotherhood, of course.

New Thought

New Thought teaches what has come to be called "the power of positive thinking" — that man may shape his own reality with his thoughts.

Is New Thought a New Age teaching? New Agers themselves think so. Nevill Drury, author of *The Occult Experience: Magic in the New Age*, states quite openly, "From an occult point of view the power of positive thinking, which underlies many self-help philosophies, is simply white magic."[17]

Traditional-appearing religious figures have prepared

the religious public for this occult belief. Like karma, this belief tends to stifle compassion. "After all," a New Thinker will argue, "I can't *really* help him until his thinking changes."

Some extras have been added to the practice, such as using speech to "affirm" the truth of the self-created, self-desired reality. A quote from *The Laws of Magick:*

The Law of Repetition: As Crowley advised: "*Invoke often!*" The subconscious mind is impressed by repetition.[18]

Aleister Crowley, whose advice we are urged to follow, was a notorious sexual pervert and witch of the early twentieth century. (Just to give you an idea of the roots of New Thought.)

Another way to turn your cloudy thoughts into real hard cash or health or whatever is the technique of visualization. Shakti Gawain, a prominent New Ager, explains how it works.

When we create something, we always create it first in a thought form. The idea is like a blueprint; it creates an image of the form, which then magnetizes and guides the physical energy flow into that form and eventually manifests it on the physical plane.[19]

The more clearly you can picture what you want in your mind, the more powerful the force to bring it into reality. Supposedly. This is the driving force behind the "Visualize World Peace" bumper stickers seen across the U.S. (You will note that we do not yet have world peace.)

Humanism

Most people have difficulty recognizing humanism as a pagan practice. This is due to the misconception that human-

25

ism is merely a form of atheism, with no particular teachings of its own. In reality, humanism is a sophisticated form of idolatry.

In humanism, man — collectively or individually — is the center of all things. Man's needs, his wants, and his interests and judgments (as interpreted by enlightened humanist experts such as Isaac Asimov) serve as the criteria for *all* things. In other words, the humanists get to tell the rest of us what we want and force it on us.

Humanists can be religious or nonreligious. It amounts to the same thing in practice. If God exists, they say, He has left us to our own devices.

Collectivist humanists tend toward political and social totalitarianism, mostly as Marxists or Socialists. They seek the long-range evolution and betterment of society — under their control, of course.

> Religious humanism considers complete realization of human personality to be the end of man's life and seeks its development and fulfillment in the here and now. This is the explanation of the humanist's social passion.[20]

Individualistic humanists tend to seek self-fulfillment, whether spiritual or material. They seek the improvement of their own lives and perhaps the lives of a few close friends. Personal fulfillment, however, can mean anything from being a ruthless businessman to a serial killer. Humanism offers no particular moral tenets.

> Believing that religion must work increasingly for joy in living, religious humanists aim to foster the creative in man and to encourage achievements that add to the satisfactions of life.[21]

These two quotes emphasize subjective things like "realization of the personality" and "satisfactions of life," leaving everyone to define what this means to him. What if someone feels "creative" and finds "satisfaction" from being a bum or a rapist?

Feminism is humanism with "woman" replacing "man" as the center. This form of humanism holds all the same political and social goals, but emphasizes that a matriarchal society is more likely to achieve those ideals than the paternalistic society.

Humanism also includes the subheading of scientism — the inordinate worship of science. This is only true, however, when science agrees with its presuppositions. Any amount of evidence for Biblical creation, for example, is ignored.

> Religious humanists regard the universe as self-existing and not created.
>
> Humanism believes that man is part of nature and that he has emerged as a result of a continuous process. . . .
>
> Humanism asserts that the nature of the universe depicted by modern science make unacceptable any supernatural or cosmic guarantees of human values.[22]

Quite old-fashioned, these humanist quotes. They could have come straight out of ancient Greece or Rome, as you will see. In brief, humanism is simply upper-class paganism. If you're rich enough and arrogant enough, you can do whatever you want without even consulting the gods. Morality is irrelevant — or at least subject to change without notice.

Psychology

As soon as psychology is mentioned in connection with paganism, the battle flags go up. This is because modern psychology enjoys the status of a science and is so well-integrated into our culture.

Consider for a moment all of the departments of a school district that are based on one practice of psychology or another — behavioral training for teachers, IQ testing, personality tests, counseling, and dozens more. And when you realize that sociology is simply psychology applied to groups of people, you can double that number. Now think of all the people in the police department, starting with the officers themselves, who are taught and expected to use psychological training. Then think of the justice system, employment and unemployment offices, welfare programs, children's services, public relations departments — and those are only government applications.

Psychology is fed to us daily via the TV and radio. There are even counselors with phone-in advice shows. Talk shows would be a wasteland without psychologists to air their latest pet theories.

First, however, we must look at the source of this science. The two great founders of psychology were Freud and Jung — a drug addict and an occultist, respectively. Freud's addiction to cocaine is well known. Less known is that Jung wrote many of his theories under the influence of a "spirit guide," which he never recognized as a demon but labeled a "collective archetype."

The leaders of the psych world that followed were hardly better. Maslow, Rogers, and Fromm all eventually "made the trip East" and ended up involved in occultism. These three popularized the now-dominant theory in both New Age and psychological thinking that a high self-esteem is the solution to all psychological problems. They claimed that people suffer from low self-esteem and are driven to "act out" bad behavior to fulfill their unmet "needs."

One researcher, David Meyers, tested the theory that people's self-esteem tends to be low and came to the following conclusions:

(1) We are more likely to accept credit than to admit failure.
(2) Almost all people see themselves as better than average.
(3) Not only do we take credit for what we may not be entitled to (#1), we also deny responsibility for what we have done wrong.

(4) We consistently overestimate our beliefs and judgments.
(5) We more readily perceive, remember, and communicate pleasant information than unpleasant information.
(6) We overestimate how desirably we would act in certain situations, i.e., giving blood, helping the homeless.[23]

Just for the sake of comparison, we present the following chart. It shows the difference between psychology and New Age pagan teaching is often only one letter of the alphabet.

NEW AGE	PSYCHOLOGY
THOU ART GOD.	THOU ART GOOD.
YOU MUST REALIZE THAT YOU ARE GOD.	YOU MUST REALIZE THAT YOU ARE GOOD.
WHEN YOU KNOW YOU ARE GOD, THEN YOU WILL BE GOD.	WHEN YOU KNOW YOU ARE GOOD, THEN YOU WILL BE GOOD.
IN THE PROPER ENVIRONMENT, YOUR INNER SELF WILL NATURALLY LEAD YOU TO BE GOD.	IN THE PROPER ENVIRONMENT, YOUR INNER SELF WILL NATURALLY LEAD YOU TO BE GOOD.

Psychologists' hostility toward the doctrines of fallen man and sin have resulted in pronouncements that such "misbeliefs" are the *cause* of psychological problems. Many members of the psychological community consider belief in these doctrines *a sickness in itself*. In Russia they are treated that way. Pesky Christians get slammed into mental hospitals. Here in the West, psychologists often try to educate the client away from the very presupposition of right and wrong by nondirective, nonjudgmental "treatments" a la Carl Rogers and others.

Most other postulates of popular psychology are distinctly anti-Christian. B.F. Skinner, for instance, says that

29

man is so rigidly molded by his environment that he has no free will. Man deserves neither praise nor punishment for any of his works.[24] Others, like the New Thought people, say that *everything that happens to you* is a matter of free choice — poverty, illness, death. This is remarkably like the Hindu doctrine of karma.

Thanks to popular psychology, the doctrine of fallen man has been replaced by the quest for self-esteem; creation by "guided" evolution; salvation by repentance and the blood of Christ has been co-opted by the search for personal fulfillment through a wholistic life; solid godly counsel by flimsy psychological "treatments."

True science looks at things you can weigh and measure and depends on experiments that can be repeated. But mental phenomena are neither measurable nor repeatable! Has anyone ever managed to put a neurosis in a box and weigh it on a scale? Have you ever seen a paranoia complex under glass in a museum?

One of the best proofs that modern psychology has moved out of the realm of science and into the realm of religion is the fact that people continue to believe in it although study after study has shown *it doesn't work.* People who get advice and support from their friends consistently do better than people who spend $50–$100 an hour or even more for the privilege of talking to a degreed counselor.

A number of books — both Christian and secular — have categorically demonstrated the monumental and continuous failure of psychology.[25] Failure on the level that if it were a drug seeking Food and Drug Administration approval, it would be permanently banned. Yet it still maintains the cloak of a science.

One former psychologist and psychology professor told me (Paul) that while there are over a hundred different "modalities" for psychological treatment, there were really only two basic ideas: (1) Live with your guilt, and (2) Blame it on somebody else. A look through the multitude of books on the subject will confirm this simple truth. The fundamental failing here is that both approaches deny the availability of forgiveness by God through Jesus Christ. There is no hope. A fatal failure, indeed!

Psychology has even displaced Scripture as an authority in some churches. We have seen Christian leaders literally roll their eyes in disgust when a believer has, using Scripture, challenged faulty psychological concepts being touted by pagan psychologists. But it is through psychology that hypnosis, guided imagery, self-esteem (pride) teachings, pagan visualization techniques, and even past-life regression have entered the church.

Such foolishness could be the result of willful sin . . . or of ignorance. Christians today know very little about paganism. Or, to be more accurate, we know only the sanitized version recently adopted by the media and public educators. It is easy to persuade those who know nothing about the ancient empires that the New Age is new, or that certain ancient pagan techniques are the latest scientific advance.

We did not write this book to condemn, but to help. As you scramble through the ruins of ancient Egypt or the ancient Aztec empire, you will see the origin of modern New Age thinking in all its forms. You will also learn how to escape the fate of those who embraced it in the past, and what the church can do about it in the present. We hope to persuade you that the old-fashioned gospel still has enough oomph to conquer paganism, and that pagan innovations are not only unnecessary but hazardous to your health.

Now fasten your seat belts. We're off to Babylon!

CHAPTER 2

BABYLON HOLLYWOOD

Babylon, the jewel of kingdoms,
the glory of the Babylonians' pride,
will be overthrown by God
like Sodom and Gomorrah.
She will never be inhabited
or lived in through all generations;
no Arab will pitch his tent there,
no shepherd will rest his flocks there.
But desert creatures will lie there,
jackals will fill her houses;
there the owls will dwell,
and there the wild goats will leap about. . . .
Her time is at hand,
and her days will not be prolonged.

—Isaiah 13:19ff.
A prophecy concerning the destruction
of Babylon by the Medes and Persians

What has ancient Babylon got to do with the modern USA, Canada, Australia, New Zealand, and European nations? Precious little — unless you read the supermarket tabloids or the astrology column in your local newspaper; unless you have seen the movie *Star Wars* or recently donated to or attended a secular college or university; unless you are a buyer or seller of crystals and other semi-precious stones; unless your life has been at all affected by the "modern" philosophy that all religions are equally valid; unless a majority of your fellow citizens believe that the state is the proper agency to solve all social problems.

Even the White House has recently been the scene of an ancient Babylonian rite. Nancy Reagan was in the habit of consulting an astrologer — and astrology, a New Age practice if there ever was one, was invented by the ancient Babylonians.[1] Let's start there, and see how many "New" Age beliefs come straight from the ancient empire of Babylon.

Babylon, the Factory of the New Age

Today's astrologers candidly admit their debt to the Babylonians. While the Greeks refined and personalized the practice, it started at Babel. So did every type of divination and magical prediction that has been used throughout history, from dream interpretations through observations of the outward behavior and inner entrails of birds and other animals.[2]

Babylonians also invented the idea of "The Force," a pantheistic god-energy that pervades all things[3]; the worship of sacred animals, called Totemism[4]; witch-doctoring, now known in avant-garde New Age circles as Shamanism[5]; and worship of the Earth Mother,[6] which in its updated version today can be seen in feminist classes on "Women's Spirituality" at your local tax-supported state university.[7]

From Pet Rocks to God Rocks

Today's New Age is wrapped up in a theology of amulets, symbols, and talismans. The idea that such objects may contain residual powers was an important part of Babylonian thinking. Small bags of ingredients with spells spoken over them, crystals, magic shapes, words, or numbers, even body parts of men or animals were popular.

Many of these charms are being revived today. Shops have sprung up nationwide like the one in Portland, Oregon, which sells small, beaded leather bags designed to hold the ingredients for spells of protection, strength, or power. These shops also sell precious and semi-precious stones and crystals which are alleged to either contain or attract energy.

One flyer lists the stones and their magical properties. It claims, "Amethyst: Reflects the amethystine love ray of the Aquarian Age. Wearing it attunes one to love energies. Promotes development of intuitive faculties." In this, the shop owner was following Babylonian thinking, since the Babylonians extensively used precious and semi-precious stones in healing rituals, though not their chapter and verse, since the Babylonians actually used amethysts as a cure for drunkenness and gout, not as love-energy tonics.[8]

Well, we suppose that getting rid of drunkenness and gout *would* improve your "love energies." The main idea, however, seems to be that you should buy as many expensive stones as possible and wear them all at once. This is right in tune with the Babylonian spirit.

The Babylonian Hustle

The Babylonians were merchants, salesmen, hustlers. Whereas, as we will see, the Assyrians were nasty warriors with no sense of humor and the Egyptians were pragmatic sophisticates, the Babylonians believed in getting in there and *selling*. This, too, is an important New Age doctrine, as virtually nothing in the New Age is free. You pay the guru, pay the channeler, pay the swami. You pay for the Mayan wall calendar, for the mind-building session at the Universe of You shop, for the cute little images of Buddha and Ishtar. Unlike butterflies, pyramids and crystals and the Airplane Game aren't free. And you get to keep on paying forever for all your unenlightened behavior, through the magic of karma and reincarnation.

Babylon Today

But we are getting ahead of ourselves. It's time to check out exactly what the Babylonians had going for them, to see if their example is worth following.

Since all New Age roads seem sooner or later to lead to Babylon, one would expect this mighty empire to be a major world force today. After all, the New Age claims to be the latest, greatest source of spiritual power around — far superior to the "old, outdated, patriarchal" religion of Christianity, for example. With all that Babylon had going for it — mighty spells, powerful amulets, astrology, goddess-worship, shamanism, and so on — surely Babylon must be an inspiring place to visit.

Not exactly. In the words of French archaeologist Charles Seignobos,

> Near the ruins of Babylon, the only people to be seen today are a few fever-stricken wretches or Bedouin bandits from the desert, who roam the countryside looking for

travellers to rob. In the swamps of the Euphrates, a few Arabs live in huts made of reeds and mud, built on low islands which they can leave only on flat-bottomed boats, along the narrow channels they make through the dense thickets of reeds.

This land, now a desert, used to be one of the most fertile places on earth. . . . For thirty centuries, this land supported one of the largest population groups in the world.[9]

What happened? If all these New Age practices are so mighty, how could an entire empire devoted to them fall so low?

Babylon Yesterday

Actually, we should have asked, "How could *several* empires devoted to them fall so low?" For Babylon was the site of two major empires and a number of minor ones.

During the first two thousand years of its history, Babylon was ruled by "a succession of kings, of whom we know nothing, often not even their name."[10] This is not exactly true, since the Bible names Nimrod, great-grandson of Noah, as the founder of Babylon and the other major cities in Shinar, and also the major cities of Assyria, including Nineveh and Calah, both of which have been discovered and excavated. Babylon was one of "the first centers of his [Nimrod's] kingdom," according to Genesis 10:10.

Nimrod was the first dictator. His kingdom did not last, but his religion did. During this early period of Chaldean history, foreigners conquered the country twice, only to find that Babylon was the original ethnic and religious melting pot. Each time, the invaders ended up accepting the Babylonians' language, religion, and customs — in spite of the proven fact that the Babylonian gods had not been able to keep them out in the first place!!![11]

Meanwhile the sister city of Ur was built. Ur is important

not only because it has been excavated, thus giving us a very good look at Chaldean life of that time, but because it was the hometown of Abraham, father of the Jewish nation, which he left at the command of God. The inhabitants of Ur followed similar traditions to those of the Babylonians, including rampant idolatry and sorcery. As usual, these magical practices didn't help, and Ur was sacked (not for the first time) not too long after Abraham left.

The next great king of Babylon was the famous Hammurabi, ruling in the seventeenth century B.C. Hammurabi's Law Code is used in liberal seminaries as a textbook example of how the ancient Hebrews stole their religious ideas from the pagans around them. It does in fact show certain marks of common sense, such as punishment for murderers and thieves, but is far harsher and much less even-handed than the Law of Moses.

Hammurabi is also known for his temple-building and his massive program of canal and dike construction. Less well known are his other significant contributions to modern life — the professional army and the state bureaucracy.[12]

Hammurabi's dynasty lasted for less than a century, as northern barbarians eventually took over the area. As Mircea Eliade says, "The history of Mesopotamia seems to repeat itself; the political unity of Sumer [the land of Babylon] and Akkad [the site of Assyria] is destroyed by barbarians from without; in turn, these are overthrown by internal revolts."[13] The all-powerful gods just couldn't keep their own empire going.

Babylon continued to control Chaldea for the next four hundred years or so, but often under the yoke of a foreign king. Eventually the king of Babylon rebelled against the Assyrians, who at that time controlled the area. Sargon, king of the Assyrians, took Babylon. Babylon rebelled again, and Sargon's son, Sennacherib, decided to put an end to this nuisance. He burned the city to the ground, including its walls and temples, and threw the rubble in the canal that went through the city. His son, Esarhaddon, then made the fatal mistake of rebuilding Babylon, going so far as to lay the first brick himself.

Now we enter the period of the mighty Babylonian empire. Nebuchadnezzar, son of Nabupolassar, was the mightiest sovereign on the face of the earth. He beautified Babylon and designed its famous Hanging Gardens. He also conquered Judah and brought its people into captivity. Truly this was the proof that pagan gods were more powerful than the God of the Bible, right?

Nebuchadnezzar, to his extreme embarrassment, was forced to learn the lesson that God ruled over the kingdoms of men, including pagan empires such as Babylon. As he was walking on the roof of his palace boasting about his great achievement in building Babylon, a voice from heaven announced that God was about to execute judgment on him. Nebuchadnezzar would lose his mind and run in the fields like a wild animal until he acknowledged that God ruled over all kingdoms and kings. And so it happened. Nebuchadnezzar was reduced to the state of an animal until he learned to, in his own words, "exalt and glorify the King of heaven, because everything he does is right and all his ways are just. And those who walk in pride he is able to humble."[14]

Today the Jews are still here and the Babylonians are not. The Jewish prophets had foretold that their nation would go captive into Babylon, as a punishment for their sins. They had also foretold that Babylon itself, the mightiest empire the earth had ever seen, would be destroyed. And so it came to pass. A coalition of Medes and Persians took the city in 539 B.C. Babylon continued as a city under the Medes and Persians, but it never again would be the source of a great empire. After Alexander the Great captured Babylon — as the prophet Daniel had foretold he would — it passed through a number of hands, and eventually fell into ruin.

According to Biblical prophecies delivered more than two thousand years ago (no matter how you compute the dates of the prophetic books), Babylon will never be rebuilt and inhabited. This has most literally come to pass. And this is odd, because usually cities are built in the same sites that have proven successful in the past.

The Dark Side of Babylon

Babylon is now an *ancient* empire. Today, it is nowhere, except in the deluge of "New" Age teachings that have their roots in Babylon. The reason for this is quite plain if you believe what the Bible says about Babylon. Its religion and culture was odious to God. The Babylonians worshiped everything in sight *except* Him. They also indulged in vile practices — as usual, "The Force" has its dark side.

Chaldean sorcerers developed charms and a spiritual poisoner's art much like voodoo.[15] Self-mutilation (including castration) was a Babylonian religious virtue.[16] For the not-quite-so-virtuous, prostitution was established.[17] An interesting wrinkle on this practice was that it was *compulsory* for every Babylonian woman to become a temple prostitute at least once in her life.[18]

God had instituted animal sacrifice as an atonement ritual, but as usual, those who found God "too strict" very soon were loading heavier burdens on themselves and their children. Human sacrifice became an important feature of Babylonian religion. Consider this hymn to the god Tutu: "Thou art exalted in the heaven; in the world thou feedest on mankind; thou art princely in the earth, the flesh of their hearts thou eatest, the flesh in abundance thou eatest."[19] Those chosen for this "honor" were usually slaves, prisoners, and children.[20]

When building houses, devotees would hollow out shrines for one or several of the Igigi (the pantheon of gods and goddesses) in a wall. To protect the shrines (and the houses), they would place an infant in an earthen jar and seal the jar into the wall as a sacrifice.

41

Sanitizing Babylon

As our culture, under New Age influence, slides closer and closer to Babylon, these gruesome practices are being sanitized. It is now possible for a writer like Nigel Davies, author of *Human Sacrifice in History and Today*, a book that has been offered through major book catalogs and bookstores, to say, "Both sacrificer and victim knew that the act was required, to save the people from calamity and the cosmos from collapse. Their object was, therefore, more to preserve than to destroy life."[21] He even dares go so far as to say, "Faced with the mass brutality of our century, real as well as simulated [here he is referring to the violence on TV and in the movies], one may ask whether, in its place, man might not do better to revert to the ritualized killings of the past. Traditional [he means pagan] society catered for both material and spiritual needs; sacrifice and religious rituals . . . were a vital uniting force in the community. Human sacrifice thus played its part in man's striving to live in harmony with the cosmos."[22]

We wrote a whole book about this ancient pagan philosophy of sacrificing individuals (the ill, the elderly, children, convicts, the poor, minorities, etc.) to some so-called "higher good," and how this philosophy is being disguised and sold as "modern" ethics. It's called *Unholy Sacrifices of the New Age* (Crossway Books, 1988), and you can get it through your local bookstore. For now, let us simply point out how odd it is that total religious tolerance (as practiced in Babylon and many other ancient empires) always went hand-in-hand with human torture and sacrifice. A society that is too "loving" to condemn anything as evil ends up *sponsoring* the evil in the name of "cosmic harmony."

Playing with Fire

Many people are attracted to the New Age by flash and glitz. It's fun to play with pretty crystals and sleep under a pyramid. It's exciting to think of chatting with an ancient Tibetan Master, even if you aren't totally convinced the channeler isn't faking it. New Age books like *Communion,* the story of a man captured by extraterrestrials, read like science fiction thrillers, and there is always the forbidden thrill of all the exotic sexual practices New Agers promote.

But whoever starts out playing with crystals will end up playing with fire. All these titillating "new" ideas (new only to those who aren't acquainted with classic paganism) have agonizing consequences. Babylon didn't become a byword for its degeneracy by accident. And it didn't get destroyed twice by accident. And it hasn't remained a ruin ever since by accident.

The Jews went down into Babylon as captives — but the best of them came up out of Babylon, laden with presents from the conquerors of that land. The "narrow-minded, puritanical, patriarchal" Jews went on to flourish, whereas the broad-minded, pluralistic, sexually liberated Babylonians are no more. Their empire has crumbled, leaving not so much as a pyramid behind. Archaeologists have had to dig into the dirt to find any evidence that Babylon ever existed, and to this day no one is willing to live there.

In his play *Julius Caesar,* Shakespeare made Brutus say, "The evil men do lives after them; the good is oft interred with their bones." That certainly applied to the Babylonians. They may have invented the debased practice of human sacrifice, but their neighbors, the Assyrians, turned it into an art form. See what kind of an empire develops when a whole culture is *devoutly* pagan as we look at the story of the Assyrians in the next chapter.

CHAPTER 3

ASSYRIA, THE ARMPIT OF THE NEW AGE

An oracle concerning Nineveh . . .
Woe to the city of blood,
    full of lies,
full of plunder,
        never without victims! . . .
"I am against you," declares the Lord Almighty. . . .
        "I will treat you with contempt
        and make you a spectacle.
All who see you will flee from you and say,
        'Nineveh is in ruins — who will mourn for her?' . . .
Nothing can heal your wound;
        your injury is fatal.
Everyone who hears the news about you
        claps his hands at your fall,
for who has not felt
        your endless cruelty?"

—Nahum 1:1; 3:1, 5-7, 19

If they had a competition for Miss Ancient Evil Empire, Assyria would be the pock-marked competitor with the evil eye and the hump. Even according to the low standard of the times, the Assyrians were vile characters. Imagine Stalin with fangs or Hitler with a rattlesnake tail and you've just about got it. This probably explains why, so far, the New Age has passed quietly over the Assyrians' contribution to modern pagan consciousness.

But we can't ignore Assyria as easily as all that. Assyria was a sister nation to Babylonia, both founded by the same person and both often ruled by the same leaders. In most matters the Assyrians simply followed Babylonian customs, which as we have seen are now part of the current New Age package. But whereas modern New Agers only *visualize* a one-world government, the Assyrians *did* something about it, and for a while did it more effectively than the Babylonians.

The Assyrians were the first conquerors, as far as we know, who put their reasons for attacking other nations into writing. Briefly, their story was that The Gods Made Them Do It. As Tiglath Pileser, the most famous Assyrian conqueror, inscribed on his capital, "The god Ashur ordered me to begin marching. . . ."[1]

Today a question nobody seems to be asking our friends who dabble in contacting ancient gods, Ascended Masters, and the like is, what do you do if the god (or whatever) orders you to start committing crimes? Once people get the idea that it is their *destiny* to usher in a New Age by force (as opposed to the Christian way of gaining ground by prayer

47

and good deeds), all sorts of unpleasantness tends to develop. Like, for example, in the case of Assyria.

Crush! Kill! Destroy!

When the Assyrians moved in, there went the neighborhood. As a robot villain in an old episode of "Lost in Space" used to chant, "Crush! Kill! Destroy!" was their motto.

> Every spring, the king of Assyria commanded his troops to assemble and set off on an expedition; they would invade a region and lay waste everything in their path. . . . When the battle was over, they chopped the heads off the dead and put the prisoners in chain, often killing them, too. Then they laid siege to the capital city, looting everything within it, if they succeeded in taking it . . . they then set fire to the whole city and withdrew with their loot [and captives]. . . .
> The king was an absolute master who called himself the "shepherd of the peoples"; and indeed, his subjects did obey him just like sheep . . . the popular belief was that the god Ashur had made him king to command the Assyrians and also to subdue the kings of other nations. . . . Those who refused [to declare allegiance to Assyria] were treated as insurgents; if they were captured, they were flayed alive, crucified or impaled.[2]

The Assyrians were not in the least ashamed of their behavior. Consider Assyrian King Ashurnasirpal's own account of how he treated the inhabitants of Suru in Mesopotamia who had rebelled against Assyria. As Ashurnasirpal approached, the people became afraid and begged him to forgive them. "I killed every other one of them and led the survivors into captivity; I built a pyramid outside the gates of the city, flayed alive some of the ringleaders and had them stretched out on that pyramid. Others were buried alive as part of the masonry, while others were impaled along the ramparts. I had many of them flayed alive in my presence, and then lined the walls with their skins. I made crowns with their heads and wreaths with their corpses." The remnant were removed as slaves to Assyria, along with their cattle and the booty.[3]

Ashurnasirpal was so proud of his treatment of captives that he even inscribed the gory tales on his palace walls. Henry Layard, the discoverer of several important Assyrian cities, found this inscription, which was first translated in 1870, on the walls of the Northwest Palace at Nimroud, the Assyrian city of Calah.

> Their men, young and old, I, Assurnasirpal, took prisoners. Of some I cut off the feet and hands; of others I cut off the noses, ears, and lips; of the young men's ears I made a heap; of the old men's heads I built a tower. I exposed their heads as a trophy in front of their city. The male children and the female children I burned in the flames.[4]

The rest of the palace was adorned with similar cheery writings, not to mention bas-reliefs of people getting tortured, gargoyles of hideous demons, and other magnificent monuments to the glories of Assyria. You or I might like wallpaper decorated with pictures of flowers, but no Assyrian king was content to look at anything but murder and mayhem, even in his living room. These people were *perverts*. "Nightmare on Elm Street" stuff. Forget mousetraps — if you invented a better torture, the Assyrians would beat a trail to your door. No wonder mothers trembled when the Assyrians were reported on the march. The price of resistance to Assyria was so high, it is a wonder anyone dared resist them. Yet Assyria was fated to be humbled before the God of Israel, in spite of the Israelites' vastly inferior military forces.

Jonah and Nineveh

Few people today remember that the story of Jonah is not mainly about a man being swallowed by a fish, but really the story of a prophet of Israel telling off the people of Assyria and getting away with it.

Jonah, a hot-tempered man of God from the northern kingdom of Israel, got a message from God to go to Nineveh, the capital of Assyria, and preach against its wickedness. Jonah did not relish this assignment. He attempted to sail in the opposite direction, but God caused a mighty storm that was only stilled when the sailors threw Jonah overboard. In the belly of the fish he completed his journey to Nineveh. Immediately upon arrival he began to proclaim, "Forty more days and Nineveh will be destroyed." The Ninevites, however, instead of tearing him limb from limb, as was their custom with anyone who annoyed them, put on sackcloth and ashes, fasted, and repented. This made Jonah even more upset, because he, just like everyone else in the entire civilized world, *wanted* Nineveh to be destroyed. After all, these people were butchers! Barbarians! Torturers of infants!

God, however, had His own ideas. He had already prepared Jonah's way with various omens that had the Ninevites quaking in fear. When the prophet arrived to tell them what to do, they were willing to listen. So we ended up with the book of Jonah, the first Biblical instance of a successful mission to the heathen.

Later on the Ninevites would relapse into their old ways. But for the moment, God had spoken and they were listening.

Showdown with Israel's God

"The Assyrians came down like a wolf on the fold / With their cohorts all gleaming in purple and gold . . ." So begins a famous poem about the turning point of Assyrian history — the showdown between the Assyrian god Ashur and the God of Israel.

Sennacherib's army had worked its way to Jerusalem, subduing the countryside as it went. Now the entire country around Jerusalem was studded with the tents of the Assyrians. Inside Jerusalem, those Jews who had managed to escape the Assyrians were huddled together like sheep — and not very many sheep, at that. Now the field commander of the Assyrian army was urging the Jews to surrender, boasting that no god had ever delivered his people from the hands of the mighty Assyrians.

Hezekiah, king of Judah, asked God to avenge the insult done to His name. That night the angel of the Lord killed one hundred and eighty-five thousand Assyrian warriors. The city was still besieged, all right — by dead bodies. Sennacherib hastily withdrew to Nineveh. There, while he was worshiping his supposedly powerful gods, his own sons killed him right in their temple.[5]

Sennacherib had wisely destroyed Babylon. Esarhaddon his son foolishly rebuilt it. That, as we pointed out in the last chapter, was the beginning of the end for Assyria. From the time that Sennacherib's envoy boasted that no god was able to withstand the Assyrians, nothing went right for them. Nabupolassar, governor of Babylon under Esarhaddon's successor, allied himself with the Medes against Assyria. Together they advanced against Assyria. "Every city in Assyria . . . [was] burnt to the ground and totally devastated; none of them were ever rebuilt. The victorious armies even diverted the river Tigris through the streets of Nineveh, so that even the place where the city had once stood should be lost forever. Within a few years, no one was able to say for sure where the capital city of once-powerful Assyria had actually stood."[6]

The Assyrians' magic (and they were famous for their magic) didn't help them. Their gods couldn't save them. Yet magicians through the ages have maintained a naive trust in their power. As Charles Seignobos admits, "As late as the Middle Ages in Europe, there were incantations in use which actually used Assyrian words."[7]

Scholars today ooh and aah over Assyrian art and architecture, managing somehow to ignore its meaning (nasty death to all who dare oppose Assyria). Some are even trying to rehabilitate the culture by claiming only the Assyrian kings were crazy (we suppose then all the soldiers who obeyed the kings' order to burn little babies and skin children alive were *normal).* From this we learn a lesson: that if only Hitler had thought to build his death camps out of stone and carve statues on them, they too could be heralded as magnificent achievements of a sometimes misguided but really noble civilization.

The Assyrians believed they had a destiny to rule the earth. They visualized it, cast magic spells to make it happen, inscribed it on stone walls, and even went to war for it. If wishing could really make things happen, the Assyrians would be running things today. But their New Age petered out into the desert sands of Chaldea — gone with the wind.

The final word on Assyria is this: Assyria is gone. The vicious hordes before whom the earth once trembled are no more. God blew them away, and His people didn't have to raise a finger.

CHAPTER 4

WAY DOWN
IN EGYPT LAND

*The Lord said to Moses and Aaron in Egypt,
". . . I will pass through Egypt and strike
down every firstborn — both men and animals
— and I will bring judgment on all the gods of
Egypt; I am the Lord. The blood [of the
passover lamb] will be a sign for you on the
houses where you are; and when I see the
blood, I will pass over you."*

—Exodus 12:1, 12, 13

At-Nut stood with his family in the rich fields where his ancestors had grown wheat and flax for generations. The priests had said that the Holy Nile would soon overflow its banks and deposit the life-giving dark silt to the fields. At-Nut believed the simple ceremony had always secured special blessings on their crops. He had learned the rite from both his father and his grandfather.

Osiris, the river god, must mate with Isis, the earth goddess, in the celestial sphere in order for the Nile to give life to the soil.

At-Nut and his wife had diligently saved husks from last year's crop and, in the midst of prayers, spells, and magic words, constructed two small effigies — one for Osiris, the other for Isis. Small charms and amulets were attached to the images and they were dressed and displayed in the family altar for weeks in preparation for the word from the priests that the time was right.

After receiving the word, At-Nut gathered his children, and they began the ritual with prayers and sacrifice before the family altar. Members of the family wore their most potent amulets and symbols as they marched in procession to the spot in the field furthest from the Nile. Here they would bury the two figures together. The Holy Nile would have to extend its reach this far to reclaim the revered images of the gods — it would have to bring its life-giving silt this far.

"Let My People Go!"

But this particular year, strange things would happen in Egypt land. The despised Hebrew slaves, under the leadership of Moses, the adopted son of a previous Pharaoh's daughter, would demand that Pharaoh let them journey into the desert to sacrifice to their God. Pharaoh would refuse, smugly at first. Then would come the dreadful plagues. The Nile, the river that the Egyptians worshiped as the god Osiris, would turn to blood, killing all the fish and destroying their source of drinking water. Poetic justice, this, reminding the Egyptians of the blood of the Hebrew baby boys whom they had drowned in the river by Pharaoh's orders. Then frogs, gnats, and flies would descend on Egypt in successive waves of destruction. Next the livestock would be decimated by plague, and the Egyptians and their remaining animals would come down with festering boils. Hail would strike their flax and barley crops (which were under the protection of Osiris in his other character of the grain god), as well as every workman in the field. Then would come the most terrible plagues of all. A locust swarm larger than any that had ever come before or after would settle on Egypt and eat every single remaining green growing thing in the land. Mother Earth, Isis, would be stripped absolutely bare by these plagues from the hand of Israel's God. The Egyptians worshiped the sun-god Ra; well, Ra would fail them. Darkness that could be felt would cover the land for three days. Finally, even the son of Pharaoh, who was supposed to be a god, would be stricken, along with the first-born of all the Egyptians from At-Nut to the non-Israelite slave girls and the firstborn of all their cattle. The only families spared would be those who, following the instructions of Moses, killed a lamb, spread the blood over their doorframes, and spent the night within those doors.

Such a thing had never happened in the history of the world. Never before or since has an enslaved racial group proudly marched out of its captors' land, bearing gifts from its former masters, without needing to draw a sword against them. Never had the gods of a nation been judged so thoroughly as the gods of Egypt — the same gods New Agers are trying to revive.

Egyptian Religion

The sun hammers down on the contrasting soils of Egypt. A comparatively thin strip of very fertile soil bordering the Nile River cuts a lively swath through the sterile desert sands. The yearly influx of the Nile overflowing its banks and leaving rich silt deposits planted a rhythm of nature in the minds of the Egyptian people. The River, The Earth, and The Sun became the major gods of Egypt. But those were about the only consistent things about their religion.

Egyptians never developed a coherent theology. Their spiritual life was guided by a combination of old village tales and minor gods. As often as not, the stories conflicted. This resembles today's New Age movement where reality is supposed to only be an illusion and absolutes disappear.

When Egypt became more politically unified, a priestly guild arose. The priests overlaid the religious confusion with several main teachings which revolved around Ra, the mostly inactive sun god, and the story of Osiris, the Nile god, and his sister-wife, Isis, the earth goddess. The other important doctrine was that of the elevation of the Pharaoh to the level of a god — the son of Ra. This set the doctrine of state-worship in concrete in a way that had not been attempted even by the Assyrians and Babylonians, whose kings had been merely the favorites of the gods, not their children.[1]

Religion and State among the Egyptians were completely identified. God himself was the ruler, and the king was his son. The temples were but the houses of prayer for the king, which none but him and the consecrated priests could enter.[2]

This separation between the people and the god (Pharaoh) who ruled Egypt caused difficulties for the state religion. The common folk felt little affinity with the aristocratic gods and government. It didn't take long for the priests to see the value of integrating popular religion and its practices into their official teachings. Soon Egypt boasted a multitude of gods and goddesses — one for every conceivable plant, animal, or insect. The divine couple of Osiris and Isis formed the centerpiece.

The incestuous marriage of Osiris to Isis was further complicated by the introduction of Osiris' brother, Set, and Set's wife.

Nephithis was the wife of Set, and greatly resembled her sister Isis in character. She was also called the mother goddess and the mistress of heaven. She bewailed the murdered Osiris [killed by Set], and is guardian of the pious dead. She becomes by Osiris the mother of Anubis, whom Isis adopts and brings up, while, on the other hand, Isis is sometimes designated as the wife of Set. [3]

This ancient soap opera gives new meaning to the phrase, "keeping it in the family."

Today Set, the Egyptian god of evil, has been revived as a god under the auspices of the Temple of Set, a Satan-worshiping cult, and Isis is the centerpiece of both TV shows and serious worship. The Rosicrucian Order claims to trace their roots to this ancient Egyptian mystery religion. One New Age promoter, Dr. Toby Weiss, offers to help you "explore inner Egypt" by a "Power Places Tour" where you "travel back into ancient Egypt to experience the Gods/Goddesses and their sacred temple sites.[4] Weiss claims to lead "many people into their own initiation into the inner essence of Egyptian life."

The Egyptian fascination with amulets and symbols is still with us today. The ankh appears frequently today as jewelry and is prominent in New Age literature and paraphernalia. The eye of Isis's son Horus (he only had one eye, Set having destroyed the other) has become another popular symbol in modern paganism.

Osiris, however, is not terribly popular, which is not surprising in our cowboy civilization. Osiris was definitely the wimp of the gods. As the story goes, Set captured Osiris and cut him into thirty-six pieces, scattering them around the earth. Isis tracked down most of them and managed to fix Osiris up enough to get her pregnant with Horus, but not enough so he could move around or speak or anything like that. Like the Canaanite god El, this put Osiris conveniently out of the picture, so younger gods could take over.

Although Osiris and Isis are strikingly similar to the other god/goddess combinations in other cultures, the Egyptians at first took the position that the sexual rites, so common in Baal/Ashteroth worship, were reserved for the initiates into the priesthood.

> So the people watched as the seal on the door leading into the holy of holies was broken. They gazed in wonder while the awesome priests entered the sanctuary to pay homage to the god who occupied a throne hewn from a massive granite block. As the doors swung shut behind these privileged few, the masses turned and left, each carrying with him his own thoughts of Osiris. . . . Gradually the sexual aspect of the great god persuaded the people to include the phalli in their public ceremonies, and to emphasize the symbols ever more frequently in their festivals. . . .[5]

Osiris/Isis worship eventually degenerated into the pagan orgies seen in other lands, probably driven by the people's jealousy over the libertine indulgences of the priests. It was not enough for them any longer to have their popular religion recognized; they wanted to participate in the "mysteries."

Marcus Bach points out:

> The first Isis was the "Veiled One," the concealer of hidden truth. Her naked form was draped with scarlet cloth. Her right breast was a cluster of purple grapes, a hint of the lust of man's eternal passion; her left breast was a sheaf of wheat, symbolizing that in the grain is hidden the sperm of life. The priests said all this was high and noble meaning, but the disenfranchised multitudes made her a courtesan. . . .
>
> Osiris became a confused and divided figure. Sex was his emphasis and sexual orgies were introduced until he was once more dismembered, not by cruel Set [as in the myth], but by the priests and the people. . . .
>
> Disenchanted, the people turned to anything or anyone who would bring them good fortune, whether it was an ankh, an Apis, or an ordinary animal. The priesthood, as well, began to doubt the heretofore unquestioned power of their god. Then strange things happened. The man in his field realized that his grain grew just as well without the corn god's aid; the masses, convinced that Osirism was but an excuse for licentiousness, turned their rituals into unabashed sexual orgies. The priests, degraded by rumors that they, too, held indecent sexual ceremonies in secret chambers of the temples, found themselves shorn of any holy illusion so far as their once awed worshipers were concerned. [6]

Pharaoh Akh-en-Aton tried to reform matters by elevating his personal sun cult to a new state religion. Some have speculated that this was a form of primitive monotheism similar to (and perhaps influenced by) Jewish monotheism. But it was more like a return to Babylonian pantheism. The Babylonians described God in terms of a life force but still accommodated a pantheon of gods. Akh-en-Aton's reform died with him, in any case, and Egypt plunged back into licentiousness.

In whatever form, Egyptian pantheism led to degeneracy.

> This pantheism told on Egyptian morality. The ethical system was practically destroyed. . . . If everything be an emanation from God, and hence part of God, then sin is impossible. This was a hopeless fall, and resulted in those features so disgusting to Jews, Greeks, and Christians.[7]

Egypt, once the mightiest nation on earth, by the time of the fall of Jerusalem to the Babylonians was reduced to the state of a "reed which pierces a man's hand . . . if he leans on it!" (2 Kings 18:21). It would enjoy a brief renaissance under Cleopatra, thanks to her intrigues with Roman leaders, but was doomed thenceforth to dwindle to its present status of a third-rate world power, with the native Egyptians ruled by Arabs. Osiris was finally exported to Greece as Dionysus and to Rome as Bacchus — two hedonistic gods who greatly aided the destruction of their various cultures. In Egypt, native Egyptian religion itself has been wholly replaced by Coptic Christianity and Islam.

The pyramids sit crumbling in the desert. Their treasures have been extracted and carried around the world for the amusement of museum crowds. The native Egyptians are ruled by Arabs whose religion has nothing but contempt for the gods of Egypt. Still the Egyptians' "words of power,"[8] their *Book of the Dead,* and even their gods are being revived as the latest and greatest spiritual forces. It begins to look like the New Age has an obsession with failure.

CHAPTER 5

IN CANAAN LAND (IT'S NOT SO GRAND)

Then the Lord said [to Moses]: "I am making a covenant with you. Before all your people I will do wonders never before done in any nation in all the world. The people you live among will see how awesome is the work that I, the Lord, will do for you. Obey what I command you today. I will drive out before you the Amorites, Canaanites, Hittites, Perizzites, Hivites and Jebusites. Be careful not to make a treaty with those who live in the land where you are going, or they will be a snare among you. Break down their altars, smash their sacred stones and cut down their Asherah poles. Do not worship any other god, for the Lord, whose name is Jealous, is a jealous god."

—Exodus 34:10–14

For miles the tents spread over the desert. People milled about them: warriors trying on their armor, women chasing small children, girls carrying water to the flocks. Even from a distance the people radiated strength, health, and youth. Not an old man was to be seen — every one of that generation except for Joshua and Caleb had perished in the wilderness.

In the middle of the camp, above the Tabernacle, a pillar of cloud sheltered the people from the force of the blistering noonday sun. Balak's spies watched them, trembling, and then scrambled back to tell their master, king of Moab, the dreadful news:

"The Israelites have come!"

Before the next ten years were over, every tribe in Canaan would have felt the heavy hand of God's people. Yet those Canaanite tribes had cities "fortified up to heaven" and manned by strong armies. Some of the people who lived there were giants. The land was full of witches, sorcerers, and worshipers of supposedly powerful gods. Mother Nature was courted and appeased — no strip mining in Canaan! The Canaanites had amulets, charms, spells, and idols to fall back on, and were as sexually liberated as the writers of *Hustler* magazine could wish.

So how did the Israelites, who lacked all these New Age advantages, conquer the land?

The Iniquity of the Amorites

The answer of *how* the Israelites conquered Canaan is the same as the reason *why* the Israelites conquered Canaan. As the King James Version of the Bible so eloquently puts it, the iniquity of the Amorites (the chief tribe of Canaan) was full. It had not been full in the time of Abraham, and therefore God had refused to give him the land at that time (Genesis 15:16). But now the Canaanites had rotted. They were not only sinning, but had glorified and institutionalized their sins. Even tiny children and animals were used for their lusts. They had become as "modern" as God was going to let them.

People like to complain that the Old Testament God was "unloving and harsh" for commanding the Israelites to destroy the Canaanites. Such people ought to watch some of the older movies that dealt realistically with paganism before it became the fashion to glamorize it. In *Tarzan, the Ape Man,* for example, little black dwarfs capture Jane, her father, and the rest of their party. Then the little men drag them to a hut, where the captives are thrown one by one to a giant gorilla, who tears them to pieces and eats them alive. The dwarfs sit in circles, watching this and gibbering with glee, rather like the crowds in Rome used to delight in the slaughter of humans in the gladiatorial ring. Their enjoyment of the suffering of the black bearers is absolutely disgusting to watch. When Tarzan sends the elephants through to stomp on these gruesome little savages, ninety-nine out of one hundred moviegoers are glad to see it. Such evil cries aloud to be destroyed.

Today the state has the job of punishing evildoers with the sword, and the church has the job of trying to save their souls. God's people will not ever again be formed into armies to conquer pagans with the sword. But if you would like to try to understand why the Israelites were righteous back then in destroying the Canaanites, instead of imagining devout, nature-worshipping pagans with flowers in their hair, realize we're talking about entire tribes of child molesters, cannibals, and people who delighted in watching helpless human beings suffer.

Until recently, the Western nations believed in executing

such criminals. Only under the influence of Easternized psychology (which has been the back door for introducing paganism to the West) has this concept of justice been replaced by the concept of "rehabilitating" such criminals and letting them loose to commit their vile crimes again and again.

This should tell us that we are closer to Canaan Land (old, bad Canaan) than we think.

It took time, though — hundreds of years — before the tribes of Canaan degenerated to the point where God could righteously unleash the Israelites on them. And the fall of Canaanite religion is instructive for us today.

El v. Baal

For centuries the battle of the gods raged in Canaan. Both Baal and El vied for the worship of the people.

El was a kind, generous god — the last remnant of the Canaanites' memory of the God of Noah. Over the years that memory had slipped into pagan distortion, and El acquired a wife and a pantheon of lesser gods to alternately help, then harass the old gentleman.

El was called "creator of heaven and earth" and yet, during the Israelites' stay in Egypt, it seems that the younger, more virile Baal stole the hearts of the Canaanite people. Not only that, Baal also stole the heart of El's wife, Ashteroth. Finally she dumped El for Baal.

The God of Sun and Sex

And what a contemporary god Baal was! Marcus Bach describes him as "the god of sun and sex."[1] Give Baal a tan and a surfboard and he would be able to step into the twentieth-century, Southern California beach scene.

Throughout the shrines or groves erected to Baal, the sun

god, and Ashteroth, the earth goddess (his mother/wife), stood obelisks of obvious phallic character. The tribes of Canaan were completely, 100 percent obsessed with every kind of deviant sex, from temple prostitution of both girls and boys to incest and bestiality.[2] Modern sociologists of religion like to refer to the "devout" nature of these beliefs.[3] They mean that the Canaanites sincerely believed that these practices were approved by the gods. That, of course, justifies the Nazi death camps and every other horror of history, since the more evil the deed, the more likely the doer is to justify it.

Today both *Playboy* types and modern feminist goddess worshipers would love to reintroduce Baal-like thinking. One such female, Barbara G. Walker, author of a book inappropriately titled *The Skeptical Feminist*, recommends mandatory sexual initiation of young boys and girls by older men and women in specially designated "Love Temples." In her thinking, adding religious overtones would justify this child-molesting. At least she is honest enough to point out that such "modern" sexual "liberation" really harkens back to the ancient goddess worship of thousands of years ago.

> Such official sex education occurs in a religious or semireligious setting, because sex is viewed as a solemn sacrament. . . .
> Love Temples are founded on much the same rationale as were ancient shrines of the Great Mother.[4]

The goddess rites of Ashteroth were inseparable from those of Baal. Again, as with Ishtar in Babylon (note the similarity of the names Ishtar/Ashter), the goddess had a bad case of sexual identity crisis. Some of the priests appeared in women's garb during the yearly celebrations.

> The Moabites made her a male divinity, and Dilbat, the planet Istar [Ishtar or Ashteroth] was "a female at sunset

and a male at sunrise" — a "maless" would be the English imitation of the artificially-coined word. She is even made the sun-god himself. [5]

So too, sexual confusion is prized in today's New Age utopia.[6]

When the deified couple were both honored at the same time, the only word for the "worship" is *gross*. Even the blasé Greeks were aghast. The ceremonies included gluttony, drunkenness, fornication, and incest — and *everyone* participated.[7] Then there was the priestly self-mutilation, copied from Babylon:

> If the land was dry or if a drought ensued, the priests enacted other mimetic rites, simulating rain by slashing their bodies with knives until the blood gushed out. This was to show Baal how he should pour rain upon the fields. Meanwhile, they chanted,
>> Where is the victor Baal,
>> Where is the prince lord of the earth?
>> The virgin earth is awaiting him![8]

Baal's title *Baal-Phegor* — "lord of licentiousness" — was an understatement. He was personally involved in acts of deviant sex, thus justifying them for his worshipers.

> The ancient Middle East made a place for homosexuality and bestiality in its myths and rites. In the Asherah cult the . . . priests had a reputation for homosexual practices, even as the . . . priestesses for prostitution. Israel eventually banned both . . . while in Ugarit [they] were priestly guilds in equally good standing. Baal is portrayed in Ugaritic mythology as impregnating a heifer to sire the young bull god. The biblical book of Leviticus (18:22–27) bans homosexuality and bestiality expressly because the Canaanite population had been practicing those rites, which the Hebrews rejected as abominations.[9]

Nor was his consort, Ashtorah/Anath, any better. Unlike the popular sanitized image of fertility goddesses, Ashtorah was cannibalistic and vicious. Consider this revealing extract from the section on Canaänite religion in the *New Encyclopedia Britannica:*

> In order to celebrate the victory [of Baal] over the Dragon, Anath gives a banquet in Baal's honor. Soon after, the goddess shuts the doors of the palace and, succumbing to homicidal fury, falls to killing the guards, the soldiers, the old; in the blood that rises to her knees she girdles herself with the heads and hands of her victims. The episode is significant. Parallels to it have been found in Egypt and especially in the mythology and iconography of the Indian goddess Durga. Carnage and cannibalism are characteristic features of archaic fertility goddesses.[10]

Baal was Canaan's most popular export. His sexual revolution was immensely widespread then, as it is now. As Marcus Bach noted, " . . . the popularity of the god of sun and sex attracted other Semitic tribes from far beyond its borders."[11]

In keeping with the general New Age practice of taking ancient pagan teachings, zapping on some ecological or sociological buzzwords, and calling the result "New," old-fashioned pagan religious sex is making a comeback. We have already heard from Barbara Walker and her invention of "Love Temples." Antero Alli takes the ecological angle. He begins an article entitled "Man/Woman Planet"[12] with the bold (some would say nutty) assertion, "The Earth is a living, breathing entity that has chosen to incarnate as this planet." From here he claims that "feeding the planet" is necessarily done through "a certain kind of man-woman relationship serving to generate bio-psychic energies." He means *sex.* But not just *any* sex — it must be between specially selected couples which "the planetary intelligence" selects through "signals from the DNA matrix."

Alli claims that all this "feeding the planet" takes place with complete disregard to conventions like "Romance, Marriage, Having Babies, and Buying Furniture." In other words, wiping out civilization and the human race would "feed" the dirty old lady, Mother Earth. This puts humans on a lower level than sparrows, who in Alli's own terms Court, Have Babies, and Build Nests.

Even the ancient orgiastic rites weren't enough to satisfy Baal. As usual when men and women turn sex into an excuse for orgies, the *products* of that sex — namely, their own children — began to be sacrificed to the god of their lust. It is here that we see why the God of Israel cried out through His prophet Jeremiah.

> "For they have forsaken me and have made this a place of foreign gods: they have burned sacrifices in it to gods that neither they nor their fathers nor the kings of Judah *ever* knew, and they have filled this place with the blood of the innocent. They have built the high places of Baal to burn their sons in the fire as offerings to Baal, something I did not command or mention, nor did it enter my mind. So beware, the days are coming, declares the Lord, when people will no longer call this place Topheth or the Valley of Ben Hinnom, but rather the valley of Slaughter." [13]

> Even children were sacrificed; they were put into a leathern bag and thrown the whole height of the temple to the bottom, with the shocking expression that they were calves and not children. [14]

The God, Jehovah, who was also called El, was a more formidable opponent for Baal than the El he had defeated in earlier times. *This* El was the Real Thing, not just a corrupted memory of the God of the fathers. *His* prophets had power.

Baal v. the Real God

Baal's province included rain and lightning. So it was quite a kick in the face for him when God told Elijah to say that it would not rain until he gave the word, and the rain ceased for three and a half years. Nor was that the last of Baal's embarrassing moments. At the end of those years Elijah challenged King Ahab and Jezebel to send "450 prophets of Baal and 400 prophets of the Ashterah [Ashteroth], who eat at Jezebel's table," to meet him at Baal headquarters — Mt. Carmel.

> And Elijah went before the people and said, "How long will you waver between two opinions? If the Lord is God, follow him; but if Baal is God, follow him." But the people said nothing.[15]

The Bible tells how Elijah delivered God's challenge to the priests of Baal to have *their* god (the god of rain and lightning) kindle the fire under his own sacrifice. When their prayers failed and Elijah mocked their failure ("Perhaps he is asleep. You better call louder!"), they became frantic and began to cut themselves. As we have seen, this account is right in line with the historical evidence of how Baal's priests behaved.

Elijah's prayer brought down such fire from heaven that even the stones were consumed. The people were no longer speechless. "The Lord, He is God!" they cried over and over. The priests fled in terror, but the people seized them and they were slain. Hours later, Elijah prayed again and the rain was restored. In the pitched battle between El and Baal, El was the clear and undisputed winner.[16]

Did God Evolve?

Biblical critics have tried to imply that the worship of Jehovah was merely an evolutionary growth from the worship of other Canaanite deities — perhaps just a more sophisticated version of the old El that had been defeated by Baal. But Ulf Oldenberg has done an in-depth study of the region's religions — and specifically the conflict between Baal and El — and has concluded, "The more I studied pre-Israelite religion, the more I was amazed with its utter depravity and wickedness. Indeed there was *nothing* [emphasis his] in it to inspire the sublime faith of Yahweh. His coming is like the rising sun dispelling the darkness of Canaanite superstition."[17]

Indeed. Developing Biblical doctrine and practice from the Canaanites would be like Christian morality evolving from the pages of *Hustler*. It simply can't be done.

Israel was not just a little bit different from the other nations when she was following the Lord — she was going 180 degrees in the opposite direction. Unhappily, Israel (and her sister nation, Judah) doomed herself by making the same fatal mistake about the Canaanites that the church is now making about the New Age. We will find out what it was in the next chapter.

CHAPTER 6

JERUSALEM BABYLON

*"Be careful not to make a treaty with those
who live in the land [of Canaan]; for when
they prostitute themselves to their gods and
sacrifice to them, they will invite you and you
will eat their sacrifices."*

—Exodus 34:15

Ahiam rushed into the house, his arms full of wood. His mother looked up from the kneading trough and cursed. "By Ashtoreh! Surely you should have been back an hour ago! I have had to knead this dough one extra time, waiting for you!"

"Sorry, Mama." Ahiam danced away from her slapping hand and out into the courtyard, where his father was clearing away the ashes of the last fire. His little sister Maacah toddled out to watch. She was his only sister — baby Jerusha had been given as a gift to the great god Molech in a special ceremony in the valley of the sons of Hinnom that only the grownups attended. It was good that his parents had done so — now their family was sure to have good luck, and besides, one baby sister was enough.

Soon Papa would light the fire to bake Mama's cakes that she had made for the Queen of Heaven. All down the street he could see other families doing the same. It was the way it had always been, as long as he could remember, in the city of Jerusalem.

> ". . . See if there has ever been anything like this: Has a nation ever changed its gods? (Yet they are not gods at all.) But my people have exchanged their Glory for worthless idols."[1]

With these words from the mouth of Jeremiah, God indicted Judah. None of the idolatrous nations had ever abandoned their gods, no matter how powerless they proved in time of need. Yet Judah had traded the true God for stocks of wood and pillars of stone. They were sacrificing their own children to these idols. In a few short years, God would show His terrible judgment on these practices by delivering His own people over to the Babylonians. Only one-third would survive the horrors of the plague, the sword, and the siege. These would be dragged out of their own land and taken as despised captives into the country that was the world center of paganism.

God would in time judge the Babylonians and call a remnant of His people back to their own land, but only after they had developed a total disgust of idolatry. In the meantime, those who had run after foreign gods would suffer horribly for their choice, as once again the foreign gods proved utterly unable to save them.

What brought the chosen people of God to the lowly position of slaves in Babylon? How did they come under the control of pagans, after having tasted the joys of freedom?

How was Biblical Israel conquered by the Babylonian New Age?

Addicted to Idolatry

When God delivered Israel from slavery in Egypt, He sent plagues to judge Osiris and Isis, the Egyptian version of Baal and Ashteroth, and afflicted the entire land. Then He miraculously made a division between Goshen, where His people dwelt, and the rest of Egypt. The remaining plagues never touched Israel. Wondrous works followed miracles, and finally Yahweh divided the Red Sea and allowed the millions of Israelites to cross on dry ground as the waters formed "a wall on the right hand and the left."

Yahweh finally judged the "living god" of Egypt, Pharaoh, by crushing him under those collapsing walls of water.

But it wasn't long before the Israelites' hearts were as hardened to the power of God as Pharaoh's ever had been.

When Moses was called up on the mountain for further instructions from Yahweh, they called on Aaron to make them a god such as they were used to — one that could not see or hear — one that was worshiped with drunkenness and debauchery — one like Osiris.

Since deities of power in the ancient world were often represented as bulls, Aaron fashioned a bull for the people to worship. The frantic sounds of music greeted Moses as he wound his way down through the crags of Sinai with God's gift for Israel, the graven tablets of the Law. Moses was angry. He knew the Israelites were practicing idolatry — God had told him. He had begged God for their lives, but when he actually *saw* the debacle, he flung down the tablets and asked crying, "Who is on the Lord's side?"

When some of the Levites responded to Moses, he sent them out to slaughter almost three thousand people — and the Lord also plagued the people.

But that entire generation of adult male Israelites did not learn. All except for Joshua and Caleb died in the desert.

Compromising with the Canaanites

It took forty years for the Israelites to make the short trip to Canaan — long enough for their children to grow up fearing the Lord. Then, just before they were about to enter Canaan, Moses once more reminded them to keep completely separate from idolatry.

> "Obey what I command you today. Behold, I will drive out before you the Amorites, Canaanites, Hittites, Perizzites, Hivites, and Jebusites. Be careful not to make a treaty with those who live in the land where you are going, or they will be a snare among you. Break down their altars, smash their sacred stones and cut down their Asherah poles. Do not worship any other god, for the Lord, whose name is Jealous, is a jealous God. Be careful not to make a treaty

with those who live in the land; for when they prostitute themselves to their gods and sacrifice to them, they will invite you and you will eat their sacrifices. And when you choose some of their daughters as wives for your sons and those daughters prostitute themselves to their gods, they will lead your sons to do the same. Do not make cast idols."[2]

God had promised to completely destroy the inhabitants of Canaan. He commanded a clean sweep so that Israel would be free of all Canaanite influence. God continued His stern warnings against *any* associating with the Canaanites — no compromise, no mixture.

Not only did God forbid the direct worship of these false gods, He also prohibited using pagan rites as part of His worship.

And after they have been destroyed before you, be careful not to be ensnared by inquiring about their gods, saying, "How do these nations serve their gods? We will do the same." You must not worship the Lord your God in their way, because in worshiping their gods, they do all kinds of detestable things the Lord hates. [3]

God sent His angel before Israel and victory was assured.

However, when the Israelites grew stronger, they subjected the Canaanites to forced labor but did not drive them out completely. [4]

These, as one preacher has said, are some of the saddest words in the Bible. They had the strength to be delivered of their enemies — but lacked the will.

The compromise of "putting the Canaanites to forced labor" made the Israelites ambivalent about rooting out some of the more troublesome Canaanites in the valleys. It wasn't long before covenants of trade were made between them and the valley-dwellers — covenants which the Lord forbade. Then came intermarriage — and finally they accepted the whole panoply of pagan idolatry. A little leaven had worked its way through the whole dough.

As the book of Judges amply testifies, Israel's unwillingness to obey God quickly made them unable to keep control of their own land. The more "each man did what was right in his own eyes" (which by the way is a great ten-word definition of paganism), the more they suffered under foreign overlords. It was not that the foreigners were so strong, but that God allowed them to punish His people for their sins. The military strength of Israel's enemies was irrelevant; God could bring about a victory with an army of three hundred men, when He so chose.[5]

Soon it was not the Canaanites who were serving the Israelites, but the other way round.

In Israel, no sooner had Joshua and his men died off than all the land plunged headlong into the very gross immorality that was the cause of God's judgment against the Canaanites — perverse sex and ritual human sacrifice.

And thus the pendulum began swinging. One time Israel was worshiping idols and was in bondage to the Ammonites, then God delivered them by a judge; then idolatry and bondage to Moab, then deliverance by God through a judge; then . . . ad infinitum. It seemed they could not escape the cycle that their compromise had built.

Even those who wished to *appear* faithful to Yahweh often still participated in human sacrifice and other perversity — but did it *as unto Yahweh*. Jephthah's willingness to sacrifice his daughter as the result of a vow made to God is just one example of what must have gone on during this period.[6]

Yahweh specifically forbade this mixture of His worship with *anything else*. It angered Him that people would justify abominations using His name. But Israel kept on worshiping one foreign god after another — Dagon, Baal, Ashteroth,

Molech. God's prophets thundered about their "adultery," their "playing the harlot," their "whoring after other gods." There was more than metaphor in God's words — the worship of these gods was sexual in the extreme.

Attached to all of these idolatrous systems were a multitude of other forbidden practices more akin to a "folk religion," but fully accepted by the official religions.

> Let no one be found among you who sacrifices his son or his daughter in the fire, who practices divination or sorcery, interprets omens, engages in witchcraft, or casts spells, or who is a medium or spiritist or who consults the dead. [7]

Israel showed a real talent for embracing all of these abominations at once.

We Want to Be Like the Other Kids

Finally, with the last of the judges, Samuel, Israel complained that they wanted a king "like the other nations." Both Samuel and God understood the implications. Kings in "other nations" were viewed as gods or demi-gods. Israel wanted a living idol to replace God and His judges. God's pain and exasperation was evident in God's words, "Listen to the voice of the people in regard to all that they say to you, for they have not rejected you, but they have rejected Me from being King over them. Like all the deeds which they have done since the day that I brought them up from Egypt even to this day — in that they have forsaken Me and served other gods — so they are doing to you also."[8]

Idolatry Institutionalized by the Kings

After Israel got its king, David's son Solomon institutionalized idolatry when he married foreign wives against the prohibition of the Law — not to mention his own proverbs. He catered to these wives by allowing them to set up pagan gods in the very palace.[9] From this time Israel's royalty were often the leaders of the cults of Molech or Baal.

Judgment Follows

It was not long before idolatry split the kingdom between Israel and Judah. Jeroboam I, the first king of the new northern kingdom of Israel, instituted idolatry as his official state religion in order to prevent his people from making the annual pilgrimage to Jerusalem to sacrifice to the true God. This spelled d-o-o-m for Israel. In spite of all Elijah and the other prophets could do, Israel never turned back to the Lord. God sent the Assyrians to destroy it in 722 B.C. (no worse fate was possible!) and its survivors were scattered through the nations.

Judah, the southern kingdom, held out a little longer. Under King Josiah the valley of Tophet was decommissioned as a child-killing center[10] and the pagan altars were defiled. Josiah turned the valley into the perpetually burning city dump called the valley of Himmon, or Gehenna. This name became later synonymous with Hell and eternal damnation. It was the term Jesus used for Hell.

But neither Josiah's reforms, nor Hezekiah's reforms, could hold off God's judgment forever. Hezekiah's own son Manasseh was responsible for so disgracing Israel with lewd and bloody practices that God, from that time forward, absolutely refused to forgive them. The Israelites had become *more* evil than the Canaanites they had replaced![11]

When God could bear it no longer — when He would no longer put up with the insult to His name and His holiness — He handed Judah over to Babylon. The remnant of His people would learn to fear Him, as slaves in the land of their enemies.

Although God brought the Jews up out of Babylon again,

the power and glory of their nation was destroyed. Israel was the football of the nations, tossed to and fro by one conqueror after another, until they rejected their own Messiah, Jesus Christ. The destruction of Jerusalem in A.D. 70 would be the beginning of the "times of the Gentiles."[12]

CHAPTER 7

HIDDEN TEACHINGS OF HINDUISM AND BUDDHISM

*The wrath of God is being revealed from
heaven against all the godlessness and wickedness of men who suppress the truth by their
wickedness. . . . For although they knew God,
they neither glorified him as God nor gave
thanks to him, but their thinking became futile
and their foolish hearts were darkened.
Although they claimed to be wise, they became
fools and exchanged the glory of the immortal
God for images made to look like mortal man
and birds and animals and reptiles. . . . They
exchanged the truth of God for a lie, and worshiped and served created things rather than
the Creator. . . .*

—Romans 1:18, 21–25

A vast dust cloud appeared over the plain of Shinar. Tribe after tribe of fiercely proud, light-skinned Aryans were migrating from the West and settling for several brief centuries in the vicinity of Babylon.

The Aryans stood out among the Mesopotamians with their pale skin and pointed noses — which were, as often as not, held aloof from the darker inhabitants. From here, they had scattered throughout the plains and hills of central Europe. Transliterations of their proud name were to appear in places as widely separated as Ireland (Ayar-land) and Iran (Ayar-an).

Some of the Aryans, however, would move east from Mesopotamia, but not without having imbibed large portions of the religion of Babylon, "the mother of harlots and abominations of the earth."[1]

The Dravidians, the dark ancient people of the Indian subcontinent, were soon overwhelmed by the Aryan hordes, as was their random, animistic religion.

The Beginning of Hindu Religion

The Dravidians lived in terror of the spirits, and only felt some safety through following minute ritual observances in every aspect of daily life. "Holy" men, in contact with evil spirits, uttered oracles and brought the oppression of the spirit world into the family home. Amulets, crystals, icons, and colored powders served as limited protection from demons and focal points of universal "energies."

To this haphazard system the newly arrived Aryans added their own ancient tribal superstitions, now powerfully organized and energized by Babylonian religion. Local deities were soon overshadowed by the triad of Brahma, Vishnu, and Shiva — a virtual copy of the Babylonian Ea, Marduk, and Ishtar.

Hindu Racism

The Aryans viewed the Dravidians with disdain, calling them *asuras* (demons), *dasas* (blacks), *anaschs* (people with no noses), *akarmanah* (without ceremonies), *ayajuah* (without sacrifices), *adeva* (godless), *avaratah* (without purpose in life).[2] This was the first recorded attempt in human history to implement racism as part of religion. And it was successful. Even today in America where racism is almost the only universally-acknowledged sin, New Agers do not feel the need to apologize for Hindu racists. Instead, they are *copying* them.

Today New Age teaching insists that two races inhabit the earth.[3] Early in this century, Nazis, like the ancient Aryan warriors, used this occultic belief to divide between the Germanic Aryans and all other people, subjecting all others to subhuman slavery. Today's pagans ascribe the differences between the races to spiritual traits rather than physical traits. Some say that one group is descended from the warlike Atlanteans, but the more advanced spirits are those of Lemurian descent. New Age spokesman Willis W. Harmon calls this newly-evolved man *homo noeticus*.[4] The difference between the old and new races, by all accounts, seems to be in one's ability to accept all beliefs as valid — *tolerance* for ungodly religions and practices. In other words, don't upset the applecart. Don't denounce injustice. Let those in power do their thing without complaining.

Keeping the Poor in Their Place

For the last forty years India has been presented in the West as a gentle, peace-loving place where nobody would even tread on an ant. But, as we shall see, the entire Hindu society is actually designed toward one goal — keeping the Brahmin caste in power. Whatever gets in the way of this goal is ruthlessly crushed.

The superior fighting abilities of these Aryan tribes put them suddenly and firmly in command. Indian society was then divided into two castes — the free (*arya*) and the slave (*dasa*).⁵ The primary difference was based on skin color. This obvious prejudice was justified by the twin doctrines of reincarnation and karma. Later, the castes or *varnas* became four distinct groups.

> Westerners are repelled by the idea by birth one is *Brahmin, Kshatriya, Vaishya, Shudra,* or outcaste. Hindus may remind Westerners that a *Brahmin* is not a *Brahmin* because of his birth but rather his birth into a *Brahmin* family was a result of his having attained that status by reason of his reincarnations. *Varna* is determined by *karma*. Birth into a *varna* is no accident. It is the natural result of karmic causes. ⁶

As a man is continually reborn, it was said, he is born into the caste he deserves because of the good or evil done in his past. His troubles are his own doing — a cosmic survival-of-the-fittest. Chris Griscom, New Age teacher, sees this rebirth cycle as a guided trip to perfection. Along the way, he says it's OK — even beneficial — to murder other people.

> At this time, we are living with the imprint of addictions and emotional body response patterns of many lifetimes. Experience is the only way to find another blueprint. Perhaps the soul says, "You need to understand permission, so go in and kill a few people, and you will begin to understand the cosmic law of permission." . . .
>
> In that killing, the soul will begin to understand the law of permission, the recognition that the victim and the victimizer are one, the understanding that there is no separation between us. If we experience a killing in some life-

time, something in our own body is activated. It responds to that, and we get in touch with the reality that this experience is a part of us.[7]

To Griscom, it apparently is all to the good that some are downtrodden, poor, diseased, persecuted, or killed. Those are roles of the person's own choice.

The victim and victimizer are one, and we don't need to attach ourselves to either of these polarities. Rather, we need to free ourselves from the grip and the limitations of each of these roles, because they are simply roles decided upon freely by all players — agreed upon unanimously.[8]

Such callousness to the fate of the suffering is typical New Age teaching. As Shirley MacLaine, perhaps the most famous New Age teacher, puts it, "I don't care if someone mugs me on the street; I drew it to myself."[9] But, of course, she really means that if *you* get mugged on the street *you* drew it to yourself.

This leaves the afflicted "in their proper place" in the New Age, in the same way as the caste system of India. It also neatly sidesteps the possibility that the afflicted and victimized might object to their condition. If the victim of oppression objects, that is only because he is unenlightened, and his oppressors (who define what is and is not enlightenment) certainly do not have to pay any attention to him.

In India each of the four caste divisions was soon divided into millions of degrees.

The Sanskrit [Aryan] word for the traditional classification is "*varna*," and *varna* means color. But it also meant species, kind, character, and nature. Those who support the color hypothesis maintain that the light-complexioned Indo-Aryans wished to avoid assimilation with the dark-complexioned aborigines whose lands they invaded. To this day fair skin is prized in India. Almost all matrimonial

advertisements state that the wife must be fair complex-
ioned. . . . Color has long been associated with the four
varnas : white with *Brahmins*, red with *Kshatriyas*, yellow
with *Vaishyas*, and black with *Shudras*. [10]

So those relegated to the lowest class could rightly be
poorly treated — and the non-class, called untouchables or
outcastes, could be treated worst of all. Dr. Ambedkar is
quoted as saying, "To the Untouchables, Hinduism is a ver-
itable chamber of horrors."[11]

In the end, the caste system, a result of pagan beliefs,
serves as a religious excuse for ignoring the plight of the
poor and the afflicted — the very people that Scripture com-
mands that we serve.

The Core of Hinduism: Keeping the Elite in Power

Hinduism, then, does have core doctrines: reincarnation,
karma, and caste. These are essential for maintaining the
power of the Brahmin elite. To prevent the possibility of discussion as to whether these doctrines are true or false, Hinduism also cleverly presents itself as a supermarket of
beliefs. You can believe anything you want to and worship
any god of your choosing, so long as you acknowledge the
sacred Brahmin caste.

The Brahmins were quick to exploit their position as the
priestly caste.

By the time of the *Brahmanas* (c. 800–700 B.C.) the Brahmins
had become a hereditary priesthood in charge of all
sacrificial duties, for which they were paid fees by the people. The Brahmins were now suggesting that by the right
sacrifices, which they alone could offer, they could procure
the favours of the gods, various temporal blessings, and a
good place in heaven. Gods, men, governments, all were
under priestly control. . . .

The fruit of this control became increasingly hard to bear, as the priests loaded heavy burdens on the people. In India, as in other places, challengers to the elite appeared in the sixth century B.C.[12]

> In the sixth century BC there was a tidal wave of revolt against the priestcraft of the ancient world. This wave shattered the power of the old religions, though their cults continued to exist as backwaters for centuries. Seven world religions appeared within fifty years of each other and all continue to this day [Zoroastrianism, Judaism, Buddhism, Jainism, Confucianism, Vedanta Monism, Taoism]. . . .
>
> The first causes of this great movement are probably as complex as the Renaissance and Reformation in Europe 2,000 years later. One obvious possible source is the preaching of Isaiah (c. 740 B.C. onwards) and the other eighth-century prophets of Israel, with the refrain from Jeremiah and Ezekiel a century or so later. Certainly we can find most of the ethical emphases of Zoroaster, Buddha (c. 563–483 B.C.), Mahavir (599–527 B.C.) and Confucius (551–479 B.C.) in the great prophets. . . .
>
> The actual spark may or may not have come from Israel via Persia, but it is significant that the revolt was simultaneous in both India and China.[13]

Like a cobra, Hinduism was able to finally open its mouth wide enough to swallow all these contenders. We will see how it did so in a minute. Right now let's take a look at the *real* teachings of Hinduism — every one of which is now accepted as a New Age doctrine.

Escape from Reincarnation

The goal of Hinduism is to finally exhaust the reservoir of karma and become one with the great god Brahman — which amounts to becoming part of the void (nothingness).

Similarly, in Buddhism one desires to attain the state of *Nirvana*, to escape from the dreary wheel of life. This is called Liberation.

> In higher Hinduism, Buddhism and Jainism, man is not just interested in a better reincarnation. One life is bad enough, and the thought of an eternity of reincarnations is intolerable. The Jains offer an escape by good deeds to destroy the evil in the soul. Buddha preached that desires and passions held man in the vicious wheel of reincarnations. The Hindu Vedantists teach the release is found by union with the Absolute.[14]

> Hinduism, then, may be characterized as a system of means appropriate for the attainment of Liberation. . . .
> The nonliberated man is subject to common destiny: enslaved by his actions which follow him indefinitely, "as a calf follows its mother," he is condemned to be reborn; and as most human actions are tainted with malice, the risk of being reborn in a lower condition, ultimately as an animal, is greater than the possibility of achieving an exalted state. [15]

New Age teachers generally do not focus on the undesirableness of reincarnation. By promoting both reincarnation and the search for nirvana at the same time, they manage to appeal both to the desire for special knowledge and the desire to escape God's judgment. They also do not stress the possible negative consequences of reincarnation.

All New Agers seem to expect to be President in their next lives. Why not? At least several thousand of them have been Cleopatra before!

The Sexual Revolution

Some Hindus try to reach nirvana by assiduous navel-gazing. Others hope to party their way to liberation.

A look at ancient Hindu temples immediately reveals the intense saturation of sexual themes running from simple phallic images of veneration to intricate carvings of naked gods and goddesses.

> The temple is dedicated to a particular god. The image of this god is accompanied by a particular attribute which can become autonomous. In the Shaivite context, for example, this attribute is often a *linga*, a phallic emblem, which is perhaps of distant non-Aryan origin. The *linga* is a short pillar of black stone, bare or engraved, around which is performed *puja* of a votive character. [16]

Thousands of years before the proto-fascist Friederich Nietzsche was a gleam in the eye of his father, teachers of Tantric Yoga had discovered the doctrine of the Aryan Superman, the man who is a law unto himself.

> The Tantric places himself above the conventional law. What others condemn, he assumes as a badge of nobility. What poisons others, nourishes him. What sends the herd to hell ensures his salvation. Hence prohibited acts are used as rungs of the ladder by which he ascends to the heights: alcoholic liquor must be drunk; meats like beef, taboo to the Hindu, must be eaten; forbidden sexuality like incest and adultery must be practiced. [17]

Tantric yoga has many followers in the West today. Not surprisingly, its proponents have found the idea of "salvation through sin" to be a convenient means of justifying evil. For example, one book which we quoted earlier suggested that one might "need" to kill (in one incarnation or another) in order to learn some valuable spiritual lesson. How handy for the Son of Sam.

Violence

Thanks to Mahatma Gandhi, a Hindu who admits he was strongly influenced by Christianity, Hinduism in the West has a reputation of gentleness and nonviolence. Hindus are supposed to be too tender-hearted to even step on an ant, let alone harm another human being. This, however, is an absolutely false picture of Hinduism.

> Extreme vegetarianism was incorporated in some sects of Hinduism, but it is important to remember that India's warrior castes have never held this doctrine. For three thousand years devout Hindu soldiers have had no hesitation about killing men in war, and eating venison, mutton, and poultry.[18]

Consider what kind of ethic springs from the doctrine that any suffering you inflict on your fellow man is his fault — he *asked* for it. If he suffers, that is the result of bad karma, his penalty for wrongdoing in a previous life. In any case, his suffering is merely an illusion that should not touch your conscience.

So India has harbored the Thugee cult, which caught and strangled unsuspecting victims as offerings to Mother Kali and the Khonds, who kept human beings to be slaughtered as slowly as possible in their nature-worship rituals. For centuries it was a *law* that widows would be roasted alive on their husbands' funeral pyre. Human sacrifice was ritualized and codified in sacred Indian books. None of this aroused any compassion until the great uprising at the time of Buddha, because, as the author of *Human Sacrifice in History and Today* says, the "underlying conditions" that breed human sacrifice were present:

> Lack of any benevolent redeemer, absence of a truly humane ethic, and, finally, belief in a ceaseless cycle of

rebirth that turned the death of man into a trivial incident.[19]

And today Hindu India has the Bomb.

Drugs

Drug abuse is another precious inheritance the West has received from our enlightened friends, the Hindus. The older among us might recall how the fad really took hold when the Beatles came back from visiting an Indian guru and began to promote drug use as a religious act. Until that time, there had been very little drug abuse in America and other Western nations.

The Rig Veda, a Hindu scripture, presented drug-taking as the greatest spiritual experience ever. One particular drug, *soma*, was called "the soul and center of sacrifice."[20]

> All the virtues of *soma* are bound up with the ecstatic experience brought on by its ingestion. . . . The revelation of a full and beatific existence, in communion with the gods, continued to haunt Indian spirituality long after the disappearance of the original drink. Hence the attempt was made to attain such an existence by the help of other means: asceticism or orgiastic excesses, meditation, the techniques of Yoga, mystical devotion.[21]

The quest for a "high" that now destroys the lives of millions of youngsters in every Western nation started right here.

Being Cool

Another nearly universal phenomenon among youth today is the desire to be "cool." In contrast with the fierce loyalties shared by Western children of the past — loyalty to family, to religious group, to community — kids today now seek to act as if they care about nothing at all. This, too, is straight out of the Hindu/Buddhist grab bag.

From 200 B.C. to A.D. 100, many Hindus were abandoning the ways of their fathers to follow the teachings of Buddha. To change this state of affairs, the *Bhagavadgita* was written.

The problem was acute. Buddha had rejected the whole idea of the caste system and the need for sacrifices as well, which meant the need for Brahmin priests. His teaching was spreading like wildfire. Even a great king of India had become a Buddhist.

The *Gita* is a dialogue between a hero of the same caste — the warrior caste — that had been foremost in the revolt against Brahminism, and Krishna, an incarnation of the god Vishnu. The hero, Arjun, is about to go into battle, and wonders why he should bother. As a Buddhist, he does not want to kill, he does not need the victory, and he feels compassion for his enemies. Krishna counters these arguments with an appeal to Arjun's duty to his caste. How can Arjun think of overthrowing all civilized society by refusing to behave according to his caste? Further, the enemy only *appear* to be people. Reality is an illusion. Thanks to reincarnation, death is no tragedy anyway. Finally, Krishna informs Arjun that he is right to not feel any desire to fight, but that he should wade out there and kill anyway. The Buddhist ideal of renouncing the world and accepting nonviolence is wrong. "Desireless action" is the right way — obeying the Brahmin rules of caste without caring terribly about the outcome.[22]

This explanation stopped Buddhism in India in its tracks. Two versions of it have also stopped the church in America in its tracks. The version for adults, *pietism,* causes Christians to care nothing about what happens to the world so long as *they* are (they imagine) saved. The version for children, *being cool,* causes them to care only about *not* caring.

Desireless action is not Christian. Jesus Christ neither established a monastery, nor called his disciples to abandon their desires. Desires were to be purified, redirected, and then fanned to intense passion. God was to be loved with all one's heart; Christians were to love one another with a pure heart fervently; compassion was to be intensely practical. . . .

If a Christian separates from secular involvement because of a preoccupation with his own salvation, he may name Christ in his prayers, but his teacher is Buddha.[23]

Demon Possession and Intolerance

"Possession" by the gods is another sought-after experience. Whether this is done through meditation, ritual dance, or other means, the gods are invited to inhabit the worshipers. Today's *New Age Catalogue* offers several books that teach you how to receive a spirit to "channel."[24]

> The worshiper, at least in the elaborate forms of cult, submits himself to considerable preparation: preliminary ablutions, food restrictions which may extend to the fast, corporal postures and gestures of the fingers (*mudra*), control of the breath, "possession" (*nyasa*) by the god of the body of the worshiper, etc. The notions of pure and impure are everywhere evident: purity is perhaps the essential watchword of Hinduism and its religious practices of purification are infinitely diversified. [25]

But what does purity mean to a Hindu? To the Tantrics, drunkenness and incest and even cannibalism are "purifying." Another group thinks that eating feces and drinking urine purify you. Still other groups regard all these things as impure. None of these beliefs is viewed as heresy.

In truth, heresy is nearly impossible in Hinduism. One of the few discernable heresies is making the claim that *your way* to Brahmin — or any *one way* — is the *only way*. Nearly the same kind of Hindu *faux pas* is claiming that there is only one God. A good example of this was a nineteenth-century attempt by Rammohan Roy at a kind of Unitarian/One God religion called Brahmo Samaj (One God Society) or The Theistic Church of India.

> The orthodox Hindus of Calcutta were furious with the establishment of the Brahmo Samaj, and organized a rival association, the Dharma Sabha. [26]

So while "tolerance" *appears* to be one of the highest virtues of Hinduism, it is only tolerance of anything that does not present Christian salvation. Rammohan Roy had not crossed the line when he touted the teachings of Jesus — so long as Rammohan continued to claim that it was not the *person* but the *teachings* of Jesus that were important. Rammohan had said, "I regret only that the followers of Jesus, in general, should have paid much greater attention to inquiries after his nature than to the observances of his commandments."

These sentiments are often expressed by New Age adherents who are appalled that anyone would claim that there is only *one way* to God. Neo-pagans are more than willing to ascribe the title of Teacher, Avatar, or Master to Jesus and to acknowledge that He is the equal of Buddha, Krishna, and others, but utterly refuse to consider the claims that Christ Himself made that He is very God. When Rammohan insisted on an omnipresent God who "is the only proper object of religious veneration," that created the furor. The local Hindus could not *tolerate* such an assertion — it was heresy.

Another doctrine Hindus can't tolerate is the claim that God is the source of salvation.

> A Hindu, even if he belongs to a group, considers himself alone to be responsible for his salvation. [27]

But even Rammohan had to admit that "Christianity, if properly inculcated, has a greater tendency to improve the moral, and political state of mankind, than any other known religious system."

This truth became more and more evident as Christianity took its tenuous foothold in India. Though the percentage of Christians in India is to this day almost negligible, the entire national mind-set was changed by their arrival. It was the *intolerance* of Christians that brought this change — intolerance of ignorance, intolerance of untreated disease, intolerance of neglect of the poor, intolerance of squalor.

> Throughout the nineteenth century missionaries poured into India to found churches, hospitals, orphanages, tuberculosis sanatoria, homes for lepers, schools for the blind, printing presses, agricultural institutes, insane asylums, elementary and secondary schools, colleges and other institutions for the improvement of the life of the people. . . .
>
> Hinduism was stimulated by Christian example to do more than had previously been done for the poor and needy; e.g., there were no homes for lepers before Christianity came to India. . . . Much more defensible [than claims that Hindus copied Christ with Krishna] is the hypotheses that the *bhakti* developments with their emphasis on the sinfulness of man and the grace of God may reflect the impact of Christianity, and there is no doubt that Christianity was partly responsible for the appearance of the great modern Hindu reformers such as Rammohan Roy, Swami Dayananda, Keshub Chunder Sen, Ramakrishna, Vivekananda, and Gandhi, for each of these acknowledged his debt to Christianity. [28]

When the English took over India, they eventually brought an end to all legally sanctioned human sacrifice including *suttee* (widow burning). The amazing courage of just one British major saved over fifteen hundred men, women, and children who were being kept as sacrificial victims by the Khond tribe in the North-West provinces. (We tell the whole story in our book *Unholy Sacrifices of the New Age!*) Through the work of missionary Amy Carmichael, temple prostitution of young girls (some only three and four years old) was finally suppressed. These were all common-place before the introduction of the Christian "heresy."

Hindus never produced a world empire like those of Egypt and Babylon, but Hindu teachings have survived intact to this day. Hindu practices, on the other hand, have been cleaned up due to Christian influence. Even so, New Agers should think twice before going into raptures about Hindu teaching, because Hinduism is the religion that has produced the poorest, most degraded and uncompassionate culture on earth today.

CHAPTER 8

UNHOLY SACRIFICES: AZTECS AND MAYANS

The offspring of the wicked
will never be mentioned again.
Prepare a place to slaughter his sons
for the sins of their forefathers;
they are not to rise to inherit the land
and cover the earth with their cities.

—Isaiah 14:20, 21,
spoken of Babylon, but applicable
to all cultures which are
the "sons" of Babylon

Montezuma hid deep in the bowels of the "Black House" where he went to practice his witchcraft. For days he brooded alone after hearing of the ignominious defeat of his warriors by the Spanish at Cholula.

For over a dozen years the Aztec empire had been repeatedly rocked by portents of doom.

It all seemed to begin after the New Fire ritual where countless human hearts were offered to the waning Sun, and the blood — food for the god — oozed in sticky waves to cover the black volcanic stone of the great pyramid of Tenochtitlan.

The warnings of doom came to Montezuma's ears from the mouths of wise men. Besides, his own eyes had seen the omens. He even attempted to disprove one adamant prophet's prediction by challenging the prophet, Nezahualpilli, to a personal match of the sacred game, *tlachtli.*

"Three games in five," Montezuma remembered confidently saying. "That will tell the winner. That will settle the truth. My kingdom against three turkey-cocks."

Montezuma remembered the rush of victory after winning the first two games. He had arrogantly strutted like a turkey-cock himself before the fawning onlookers. But then followed the agony of three losses. He felt their crushing weight even more now that the prophesied doom was upon him.

In the intervening years, while his subjects deferentially turned their eyes from his splendor, Montezuma secretly turned his eyes to the horizon in search of the onrushing destruction. Each small crisis seemed to be the one. But when he had first heard the report of fantastic cities on the sea moved by billowy clouds, he was sure.

His black arts had failed him. His treachery at Cholula had been exposed. As the leader of many military campaigns, he saw his only move was to wait — wait and see if any new breaks developed.

Doom approached disguised as Hernando Cortes.

Out of the Blue

Meteoric is the word that best describes the rise of the Aztec empire. In a few brief centuries they went from a pitiful band of outcasts from the wastes of northern Mexico to savage and sophisticated rulers of the central jungles. At first they proved useful to the established kingdoms as mercenaries. They were utterly ruthless — their greatest sales pitch. But those who hired the Aztecs failed to cover their own backs, and soon the crafty newcomers were a greater threat than the enemies they were hired to oppose.[1]

The Aztec philosophy of life was like that of Nietszche who said, "Life is essentially appropriation, injury, overpowering of what is alien and weaker; suppression, hardness, imposition of one's own forms, incorporation and at least, at its mildest, exploitation."[2]

The coming of the Aztecs seemed to be somewhat of a judgment on the superstitious and magic-laden Mexicans. All of them were fond of human sacrifice and other barbaric practices. The Aztecs came and gave them a belly full of their own way. On one occasion the Aztecs sacrificed twenty thousand human hearts in the space of four days. The black-robed priests with their eyes gleaming stood ankle-deep in the blood as it coated the great pyramid. They were only replaced as their arms became too weary to make the gash with the obsidian knife.

Cleaning the Blood Off the Ziggurat

Today the Aztecs and their fellow pagans, the Mayans, are being dug up, cleaned up, and promoted like crazy. New Age prophecies are based on the Aztec and Mayan calendars. New Agers claim to be channels for spirits of Aztec warriors. There is an Aztec exhibit, complete with ziggurat, at Disney World, and the accompanying tour talk is all about the advanced civilization and amazing achievements of the noble Aztecs. The Health Valley firm out in Montebello, California, touts its amaranth crackers as containing "The Mystical Grain of the Aztecs," and decorates the box with a picture of an Aztec ziggurat.

Even the latest edition of the Barnes & Noble mail order book catalog features a large ad inviting you to take "A Journey with the Aztec Gods." All you have to do is shell out $19.95 plus shipping and you will get a twenty-card deck of the Aztec days, a cloth bag containing thirteen wooden chips, which in combination with the cards produces two hundred sixty combinations (the number of days in their calendar) *and* a two hundred forty-page guidebook! Considering that all of this must have taken only a dollar or two to produce and that it is being sold for twenty times that much, it really is a mystery why "nothing like it has ever been offered before."

Or maybe not such a mystery. Before historical illiteracy set in, Americans used to know that the Aztecs and Mayans had two of the bloodiest, most disgusting, cruel, so-called civilized societies in the history of the earth. If anything, these Central American tribes were *worse* than the Assyrians. The Assyrians used to kill and torture their enemies; the Aztecs and Mayans did it to their own people. And in what numbers! A few examples will suffice to give you the idea of the scale on which the Aztecs operated.

Aztec society, like the Mayan and Toltec societies before it, was filled with unspeakable cruelty. Torture, human sacrifice, and cannibalism abounded on an unprecedented scale. . . .

The scale on which human sacrifice was practiced is mind-boggling — 20,000 victims sacrificed in four days during the dedication of the Great Temple in Tenochtitlan. As many as 50,000 were sacrificed annually.[3]

In months when rain was sought, a band of children were drowned, or walled up in a cave, or exposed on a mountain-top; and the more they wept, the better the augury for rain. At harvest-time, victims were thrown into a fire or furnace, and their bodies pulled out with hooks before they were totally consumed so that the precious hearts could be extracted in the usual way [e.g., by ripping them still beating out of the victim's chest]. At the periods when growth and fertility were required, the commonest practice was to behead a priestess and flay her, and for a priest to insert himself in the skin and lead a ritual dance.[4]

As Jon White, author of the book *Cortez and the Downfall of the Aztec Empire*, aptly remarked, "When we visit or study photographs of Aztec temples, we should picture to ourselves those tall staircases as they frequently appeared: covered from top to bottom with a tacky, crimson sheath of blood."[5]

Now wouldn't that be delightful on your box of Health Valley crackers or on the Disney World tour? As one of us pointed out in a letter written to the head of the Health Valley firm, using an Aztec ziggurat as a product's logo is like using a picture of the Nazi death camp at Auschwitz.

The Aztec New Age

What makes the vicious Aztecs and Mayans so terribly attractive to New Agers? Well, *they were New Agers them-*

selves! As Geoffrey Parrinder states in *World Religions from Ancient History to the Present,* "The Aztec people considered themselves to be in charge of the regulation of all earthly matters during the fifth cosmic age."[6]

Like the Nazis, who would centuries later revive this doctrine of a new cosmic age (they called it the Third Reich), the Aztecs figured that their unique position as the enlightened vanguard of a new age entitled them to throw their weight around a bit.

> As the [Aztecs], urged by their divine mission, migrated further away from their original territory towards the traditional Central Mexican cultural centers, their own culture was increasingly affected.
>
> Alien influences, both religious and social, were more easily adopted; many alien gods were admitted into their pantheon. . . . There was a considerable increase in human sacrifices, and the military men gained in power, taking over from the priests more and more administrative functions within the society.[7]

> To live was to fight. Indeed, they had early come to believe that heaven had appointed them its legionaries on earth, and to them had been given the divine duty and privilege of fighting on behalf of the gods against the cosmic forces of destruction.[8]

The peoples of central Mexico were crying out under the oppressive yoke of Aztec barbarity. To them, the Spanish *conquistador* Hernando Cortes was a savior.

Up from Babylon

The Aztec and Mayan empires are a lot closer to our own time than the ancient empire of Babylonia. From them, we can learn a lot about the original pagan religion invented in

Babylon — because to us, at least, it is clear that *the Aztecs and Mayans came from Babylon.*

Consider first the physical evidence.

Two other physical characteristics of the modern Maya suggest the northeastern Asiatic origin which they share with other American Indian groups: (1) the epicanthic eye fold, and (2) the Mongolian spot. The epicanthic fold is a fold at the inner corner of the eye which is characteristic of eastern Asiatics; it is also common among the modern Yucatan Maya. Judging by its frequency in representations of the face in sculptures and paintings, it must also have been a prevalent characteristic in ancient times.

The Mongolian spot is an almost universal physical characteristic of the peoples of eastern Asia, and is also very common among Maya babies of northern Yucatan. It is a small, irregularly-shaped spot at the base of the spine, which is present at birth but generally disappears before the tenth year. It is bluish to purple in color, which gradually fades to slate.[9]

Next, consider the similar architecture of Babylonian and Aztec ziggurats; their similar use of cylindrical seals;[10] their shared beliefs in astrology and horoscopes;[11] and the way the nobles and priests contrived great public works which the common people carried out.[12]

The more you look into it, central Mexico's ancient civilization looks like a transplant straight from Mesopotamia. The only reason secular archaeologists don't take more notice of the similarities is because they have a theory that the so-called Native Americans of both North and South America migrated over the Bering Strait from Siberia. They don't see how these people could have come from the Middle East.

Christians, on the other hand, know that the Bible refers to a time when "the earth was divided."[13] We can look at any world map or globe and see that the continents obviously once fit into one great landmass, with Central America quite close to Babylon. Whereas humanistic geologists believe the continents separated before man evolved, the Bible teaches that this Gread Divide occurred *during* human history.

Once the migrating Babylonians settled down in Central America and had enough leisure time to do more than just barely survive, they made use of the arts and social setup they brought from Babylon.

So what we have in the Aztecs and Mayans is an example of almost pure Babylonian religion, uncontaminated by any contact with Biblical religion until the time of Cortes. If ever any group of people on earth had the chance to show how noble men naturally are without the nasty fetters of Christian civilization, it was them. That is why New Agers and their fellow travelers today are sweeping the facts about these tribes under the rug, and why we need to know about them.

Highly Advanced Barbarians

Perhaps the greatest lesson of ancient central Mexico is that cultures *do not* evolve away from superstition, witchcraft, and human sacrifice. These things simply become integrated into the governmental structure and the justifications are more elaborate and "scientific." This pattern can be seen in Babylon, Egypt, and Rome, but even more clearly with the Aztecs and Mayans, who were culturally isolated.

The apparent contradiction between the fantastic gardens of Montezuma, which rivaled the Hanging Gardens of Babylon, and his utterly debased witchcraft and blood-rites takes your breath away. A complex hybridization program for plants existed among the Aztecs along with highly developed catalogs and records. The development of high-level poetry demonstrates their intellectual and philosophic range. Intricate instructions in medical texts about the proper use of carefully listed herbs reveal the painstaking efforts of scientific minds.

> These diametrically opposed attitudes toward life and the universe existed side by side — a situation similar to that of Nazi Germany in our time, where a mystico-militaristic world view and a genuinely humanistic philosophy and literature coexisted. Indeed, such a mixture of humanism and barbarism seems to be an inherent quality of the so-called rational animal.[14]

These same conditions existed in all major pagan empires — just before they fell. And, though we do not think the author of the above quote would have seen it this way, we believe that it was precisely their *humanism* (i.e., the philosophy that makes man into a god) that led to barbarism. Humanism is merely another face of paganism. And it was the pagan base of the Aztecs' civilized efforts that distorted their culture.

Only the Strong Survive

The Aztecs carefully cultivated their "mystico-militaristic world view." Their children were steeped in the teaching of evolution — a system in which only the strong survived. Children were sent to public school, where they learned of the Aztecs' destiny in the New Age of the Fifth Sun. They were also indoctrinated in the need to participate in the "wars of flowers," campaigns waged for the specific purpose of obtaining captives to sacrifice. This ritual warfare was touted as a means to prevent decadence in the young. They were also taught that the gods needed continual sacrifices as a bribe for continual blessing. Aside from that, Aztecs could believe what they wanted.

> The Aztec youth, boys as well as girls, were indoctrinated with these fundamental principles and their set of con-

nected values, as long as they were at school, from their seventh to their twentieth year, either by priests at sci-entific-religious boarding-schools, or by army officers at the less strict military and vocational schools.[15]

The assumption was that strong people improved the nation and the weak deserved their fate. An Aztec's position in life entirely depended on his accomplishments in arms. This system, out of necessity, excluded handicapped or sickly people. These segments of the population were unable to climb the ladder of success.

Combine this with a belief in total annihilation of the person and the universe as their eventual fate — a denial of an afterlife — and this led to philosophical and practical hedonism. Aztec fatalism was expressed in the poem —

> One day we must go,
> one night we will descend into the region of
>   mystery.
> Here, we will only come to know ourselves;
> In peace and pleasure let us spend our lives;
> Come, let us enjoy ourselves.
> Let not the angry ones do so; the earth is vast
>   indeed!
> Would that one lived forever; would that one
>   were not to die.[16]

In truth, this is quite reminiscent of the premature con-clusion of the writer of Ecclesiastes when he said, "Who knows that the breath of man ascends upward and the breath of the beast descends downward? And I have seen that nothing is better than that a man should be happy in his activities, for that is his lot. For who will bring him to see what will occur after him?"[17]

Much of the strength of the Aztec empire was a result of what can only be described as a warrior cult. This has now been revived by New Agers, in spite of the fact that the Aztec and Mayan warriors *failed* when faced with Spanish Catholics.[18] And not because the Spanish had superior weapons, either. The Spaniards' edge in armaments was entirely nullified by the size of the tiny expeditionary force Cortes led compared to the vast hordes Montezuma could mount. The natives' fear of the horse and gun was short-lived — and remember that we are talking about single-shot muskets, not machine guns. Aztec warriors soon learned the shortcomings of these weapons and exploited them.

> There is no question here of an urban and sophisticated society attacking a society that was merely agricultural and primitive. Two splendid and virile peoples were about to pit their strength against one another. . . .
>
> It must be remembered how thoroughly saturated the Aztec state was with the ideal of militarism. . . . The Aztec nation was permanently in arms, like Sparta, or the Germany of the Hohenzollerns or National Socialists.[19]

The central Mexicans were not weak through lack of numbers or armaments. They were weak *morally*. The Spaniards, who were no Boy Scouts, were simply astounded at the perversity of the Aztecs.

> The religion of post-classic Mexico . . . was shot through with witchcraft, sorcery and the baser forms of superstition; it was a religion in which fear and cruelty were primary ingredients. . . . The Aztec did not look forward in a mood of serenity and expectation; he inhabited a world which threatened constantly to run down or fly to pieces; his gods were not mild and forgiving but malevolent and ailing. . . . The universe was an anxious place.[20]

The Dear, Sweet Mayans

The Mayans were no better than the Aztecs. Scholars used to think the Maya were "an artistic, intellectual, cultured people ruled by priests who devoted their time to astronomy and calendar-making" and who only became warlike "when threatened by the militaristic Toltec people, their neighbors to the north. . . ."[21]

Recent archaeological and linguistic breakthroughs have, however, revealed "a darker — but perhaps more realistic — view of the Maya."[22] According to this new evidence, the Maya also waged war to acquire captives, and were in the business of sacrificing human beings long before the Aztecs.

Just like New Agers today who talk about blood "feeding the planet," the Maya believed that "blood nourished the gods and kept the universe in order."[23] Maya of all social stations regularly mutilated themselves in gruesome ways. Several experts have gone so far as to say, "Blood was the mortar of Maya ceremonial life."[24]

About all you can say for the Maya is that they were victims of the Aztecs. The big bully on the block had got himself in the grip of a bigger bully. Now the two of them were about to get the thrashing of their lives.

Judgment on the Mayans

The Spaniards were not the first judgment to hit the central Mexican tribes. Spanish Bishop Landa, writing in 1566, detailed seventy-five years of progressive judgments. First came the destruction of the city of Mayapan in a massive earthquake. Twenty-two or twenty-three years later the whole area was ravaged by a tremendous hurricane, the worst storm ever experienced there. Sixteen years later came "the pestilence of the swelling," sixteen years after that came major wars, followed by another plague twenty years later.[25]

The last plague is rather interesting. The first white men to visit Yucatan were survivors of a shipwreck. Five of them were sacrificed and eaten by Mayans. Four years later the pestilence of 1515 arrived, the *mayacimil* or "easy death."[26] Could it in any way be traced to this cannibal feast? If the Indians of North America could catch diseases from white men just by trading with them, the Indians of South America certainly had a better shot at catching something by eating them.

The Maya set the seal on their fate when their ruler and his court attempted to make the pilgrimage to offer human sacrifice in the Well of Sacrifice at Chichén Itzá in 1536. At this point, no Spaniards were in Mayan territory. They had tried twice to conquer the region and given up.[27]

The Mayan king arranged for a safe-conduct through the territory of a hostile ruler. He was a bit worried about his safety because his great-grandfather had been involved in the killing of the great-grandfather of the ruler of that territory. He and his court were feasted well, but on the last day of the banquet their hosts rose up and slaughtered them. "[This] pitted the two most powerful houses in the northern peninsula against each other. . . . This massacre, coming so shortly before the third and final phase of the Spanish Conquest, sealed the fate of the Maya. It revived old hatreds and effectively prevented a united stand against the Spaniards when they returned to Yucatan.[28]

Judgment on the Aztecs

The Aztecs had a real chance to repent — and blew it. You won't find this in most history books, but the fact is that Hernando Cortes was a powerful lay preacher. Typical of his behavior are the following examples:

> [In every city where he passed] Cortes called the priests
> and 'caciques' together and, after Jeronimo de Aguilar had
> preached them a sermon in their own tongue, he delivered
> a no-nonsense, proconsular type of speech. In the words of
> Diza: 'He told them as best he could, through our inter-
> preter, that if they wished to be our brothers they must
> throw their idols out of this temple, for they were very evil
> and led them astray. He said they were not gods, but
> abominations which would bring their souls to hell.'[29]

116

Cortez described his preaching before Montezuma and his officers in these words: "I made them understand by the interpreters how deceived they were in putting their hope in idols made of unclean things by their own hands. I told them that they should know there was but one God, the Universal Lord of all, Who had created the heavens and earth and all things, and them and us, Who was without beginning and immortal; that they should adore Him and believe in Him and not in any creature or thing."[30]

Cortez and his men did everything they could to persuade the Aztecs to abolish human sacrifice and idolatry. Their preaching met with no success. When Cortez chided Montezuma for his idolatry and bloody ways after being taken on a tour through the largest temple (where the Spanish were disgusted by the sight of fresh human hearts displayed before the idols), Montezuma replied that it would take *more* sacrifices to wash away the insult caused by Cortez's words!

Eventually the Aztecs decided to kill their Spanish visitors, these men who blasphemed the gods. But through a series of amazing miracles, Cortes's tiny band *won*. Time after time they were surrounded by huge hosts and their situation seemed hopeless, but somehow each time they were delivered.

In this judgment God was most thorough. Although the Spanish had admired Montezuma's capital city, remarking that it was more beautiful than any of the cities of Europe, they were forced to destroy it in house-to-house fighting. The Aztecs became the Spaniards' slaves, a situation that in a generation or two would be rendered much more tolerable by the Spanish priests, who protested the inhumane treatment of the captives.

From this judgment the tribes of central Mexico have never recovered. The descendants of the mighty Aztecs and Maya are still second-class citizens in the land of their fathers. Misguided attempts to revive pride in these ancient bloody empires is not what they need, but a pure faith in Christ — the faith their ancestors rejected and, rejecting, lost all.

PART 2

THE IN-BETWEEN AGE

CHAPTER 9

GREECE: THE BEAUTIFUL SIDE OF EVIL

While I, Daniel, was watching the vision and trying to understand it, there before me stood one who looked like a man. And I heard a man's voice from the Ulai calling, "Gabriel, tell this man the meaning of the vision." . . .

He said: "I am going to tell you what will happen later. . . . The shaggy goat is the king of Greece, and the large horn between his eyes is the first king. The four horns that replaced the one that was broken off represent four kingdoms that will emerge from his nation but will not have the same power."

—Daniel 8:15, 16, 19, 21, 22

"**H**i! I'm Zeus, and I'm here to help you." Words to strike fear into the heart of any Greek!

Greeks liked to tell the story of the two weary travelers who came at sunset to a town. From house to house they wandered begging for a place to sleep and a bite of food, but the unfriendly householders turned them away. Finally an old couple invited them in and fed them.

Then came the revelation!

Up from their tattered robes started the figures of the gods Zeus and Hermes. As the old people fell on their knees before them, the two gods told them that they were going to destroy the entire town, as a punishment for its lack of hospitality. The old couple, however, would get a handsome reward. They would be turned that very minute into two trees that would be pillars for a new temple of Zeus!

Hobnobbing with the Greek gods was like playing Russian roulette with a totally loaded gun. No matter what happened, sooner or later they were gonna git ya. Whether you were turned into a tree, or allowed to live forever but not to remain young, or simply deserted after the god had landed you in an impossible position, life wasn't going to be simple. If your great-grandmother had done something once to anger a god, the Fates could be pursuing you for the rest of your life. And then there was that miserable afterlife to look forward to, roaming drearily around the underworld as a shadow — *if* you were lucky and managed to escape that portion of it devoted to troublemakers and miscreants — where they were tormented night and day forever.

Naturally, when a religion has all this going for it, you will find people trying to revive it today. Whatever else the New Age may be, it is certainly a most industrious collector of failed religions. Along with the Greek gods comes a built-in bonus of marvelous classical architecture (don't look too closely at those two pillars over there!), fabulous statuary, and graceful dresses that certainly are an improvement on the current fashions.

Ancient Greece has a good image, too. The word *Greece* evokes pictures of the sparkling blue Aegean Sea and green hillsides dotted with white columned buildings. Historians admire it as the "cradle of democracy"; philosophers remember Plato's *Republic* and the tragic death of Socrates; artists pine for the days when patrons exulted in supporting the sculptors and thespians — and *everyone* seemed to be surrounded by beauty.

Greece as It Was

This idyllic image of pastoral Greece, however, is not quite the real picture. The ancient Greek city-states were not bastions of freedom overflowing with community spirit, but enforced regimes from infancy to death. Citizenship was conferred only on a small elite. The nobles of these "democracies" were the voices of the gods.

The winnowing process started at birth. Unsightly babies were exposed to the elements and the wolves, or perhaps sacrificed. Human sacrifice and ritual dismemberment abounded in Greece. Others with physical defects — those who were crippled or mutilated — were excluded from the life of the *polis*, the city-state.

If one managed to avoid all these pitfalls, he would simply be a member of the serving class — a slave — unless he were chosen for a higher purpose. The Elite, those with proper breeding and blood, could reach down and select some to serve as administrators. This class kept order. They were the guardians who carried out the wishes of the rulers, for the good of the people. But they had little influence on policy.

Even Plato's famous utopia was only a variation on this theme. It was a bit more organized, and ruthless. Plato recommended that the State choose which couples be allowed to mate. Infants were to be taken immediately from their mothers, and "no parent is to know his own child."[1] Permanent day-care was a State responsibility, and the mother went back to work as though nothing had happened. All religion and religious doctrine would be State-controlled. Education would be pure indoctrination for State goals. Music and literature would be censored so that the State's plans would not be corrupted. All things, including wives and children, would be in common. There would be no private marriage or property.

The similarities between this utopia and the utopia proposed by many New Age pagans in their dreams of a one-world government are not coincidental. In a recent visit to a witchcraft supply shop, one of us was browsing through their small lending library looking at titles about shamanism, women's religions, *The Egyptian Book of the Dead,* and other assorted occult titles. Right in the midst of all this New Age literature he found a copy of *The Dialogues of Plato,* from which he gleaned the above examples.

Prostitution of Girls and Boys

Plato's republic did not have the young girls initiated into temple service as prostitutes; nor were Plato's young men snatched up into institutionalized homosexuality as they were in the real Greek *polis.* But families in the real *polis,* for the most part, happily sold their young men into these perverse relationships. It was seen as an advancement in society.[2]

Much like today's West, the Greeks had a strong homosexual movement. In time it virtually captured the Elite and the reins of government. Homosexuality, the Greeks taught, was a higher form of love than the procreational love of a man and a woman. This was a clear denial of what Scripture taught in Genesis — that God made them male and female, not each one part male and part female. There was no androgyny or homosexuality in God's design. He did not make Adam and Steve.

In today's homosexual literature, perversity is once again being labeled as more loving than righteousness. This is done by using highly suspect statistics that are supposed to show lower violence rates between homosexual couples than with "straight" couples. They even argue that homosexuality is more loving to Mother Earth since they do not add to the population problem.

In Greece the trend of homosexual control continued until the reign of the homosexual tyrant, Alexander the Great, after which the Greek empire collapsed.

Scientism

But perhaps the most remarkable comparison between Greece and the modern West is *scientism*, the worship of "science." The Greeks were dogged about their brand of rationalism. Accepted occult practices fell by the wayside if they were unable to keep pace with what was fashionable in "scientific" advances.

Among the highly regarded "scientific" beliefs was evolution. The Greeks accepted the idea that all forms of cause and effect were applicable throughout nature — a belief called *sympatheia*. An excellent example of the outworking of this belief is the description of Greek alchemy by Luther H. Martin.

The transformative growth of seed grain into cereal was mythologized as a natural growth from the womb of

Mother Earth. The transformative growth of base metals into the nobler metals of silver and gold was mythologized as a growth deep within the ore-womb of Mother Earth, a process no less natural if more protracted. Through techniques of cultivation, the earth could be induced to produce a greater cereal yield and more quickly; similarly, alchemical practice sought to hasten an assumed natural transformatory growth of base metal into precious metal.[3]

The fact that science has disproved the assertions of sympathetic magic does nothing to dissuade New Agers' claims. They simply shift gears and say that sympathetic power comes though channels other than the physical. This effectively removes empirical and experimental science from the field since nobody can weigh and measure the spiritual plane. Thus, magic is asserted to be scientific and then exempted from scientific scrutiny — just as in ancient Greece.[4]

Out of the Mouths of Caves

The Greeks had an enduring respect for certain forms of unexplained phenomena. The Delphic Oracle was one of these. It was discovered that anyone peering into a certain chasm in Delphi would be immediately seized by a prophetic spirit and begin to utter hidden truth. It was not long before the path to the cliff was obscured by a temple and priestesses were assigned to risk the danger — for a nominal fee — of speaking the oracle.

Other forms of random prophecy were also held in esteem.

A *cledon*, an omen contained in a word or sound, was most reliable when uttered by those least capable of calculating their effect, such as fools and children. . . .[5]

New Age pagans love to appeal to the "wisdom" of children as a form of guidance for daily life. One of us knows a woman who put such stock in the random sayings of her child that she made important decisions based on these words.

Most often in the West, we hear the partial quotes of "out of the mouths of babes" and "a little child shall lead them" used to justify foolishness. But Scripture says *praise for God* comes "from the mouths of babes," not wisdom, and that the child in Scripture is leading not the nations but the *animals* — and that, only during the Millennium.

Trance channelers also take advantage of the myth that those people with least control of their minds are the best channels for granting wisdom from the gods. Yet we do not see New Age pilgrimages to mental hospitals where such wisdom should, according to the theory, abound.

As with other cultures we've seen, the downward moral spiral in Greece was accompanied by the upward cultural spiral. A rising culture does not *cause* declining morals, but increased sophistication is no *proof against* moral corruption.

Here Come de Goddess

None of this corruption would have been complete without the goddess and her perverse companions. Greece hosted two great mystery religions — the adoration of the Great Goddess Cybele (also spelled Sibyl) and the Dionysian Bacchanalia, a transplanted Osiris worship.

In both cases the *feminine* was sovereign. Priests who wished to serve Cybele were clothed and made-up as women. They engaged in a frenetic initiation dance in which they cut their own arms and bled before the goddess and finally castrated themselves — a bizarre, ancient equivalent of the sex-change operation.[6]

As for the Bacchic feasts, they were first exclusively for women but were later expanded to initiate men. The combination of wine and sex at these events led to greater and greater debauchery (a word derived from Bacchus). Men who refused to keep the conspiracy secret were tortured and killed. Stories were spread that they were carried off by the gods.[7]

Today books seriously suggest that we should revive the Greek pantheon.[8] One of us has witnessed a float dedicated to the Greek goddesses, covered with college girls dressed in flowing Greek robes, parading down the streets of St. Louis. Much New Age literature, especially of the feminist variety, invites open worship of Aphrodite and other goddesses.

But those who want to bring back the Greek gods have a strange habit of not telling us the real facts about Greek religion. So we will oblige you here with a brief recap of the glories of Greek paganism.

Nature Power

The Greeks worshiped nature, but they did not love it. Albert Henry Newman describes Greek religion as "a polytheistic personification of the powers of nature."[9]

For the Greek all of nature was instinct with life. A mountain was the sky-god's throne; worshippers went to the hilltop to pray for rain. Every tree had its dryad, and the oak was sacred to Zeus, the olive to Athene, the bay to Apollo, the myrtle to Aphrodite, the poplar to Heracles. . . . Each spring had its nymph, each river its god. . . .

Those who strayed in the country might encounter goat-footed Pan or the satyrs and centaurs, half-men, half-beasts. The sea was the home of Poseidon, of Proteus with his magic changes of form, of the sea-grey spirit Glaucus . . . of exquisite nereids, monstrous tritons, deadly sirens. . .

This affects our understanding of a number of passages in Greek literature. There is little appreciation of natural beauty for its own sake; the Greeks did not climb their

129

mountains to look at the view. Nature . . . was useful, or she was awesome and destructive. But basically nature meant living power. . . . Diotima in her catalog of beauty in *The Symposium* does not mention beauty in nature.[10]

Nature was full of capricious powers that needed to be appeased. You never knew if Pan was going to jump out at you from behind a bush or if some tree-goddess would take offense at you for picking up her twigs for firewood. As Robin Lane Fox says in his book contrasting ancient paganism and New Testament-era Christianity, "To 'follow pagan religion' was generally to accept this tradition of the gods' appeasable anger."[11]

Not all the gods were nature gods. A study of the names in the Bible shows that several very ancient patriarchs probably were the source of certain gods. Tubal-Cain, for example, who is said to be the first man to forge tools out of bronze and iron, is doubtlessly the original for the smith-god Vulcan, and Javan, one of the sons of Japheth (and the eventual ancestor of the Greek nation), could very well have been transformed into the Creator-God Jove. If this is true, we can see how literally the Bible means it when it says men turned aside from worshiping the Creator to worshiping what He created — in this case, attributing to notable ancestors the very deeds of God.

Euhemerus, an ancient Greek writer who studied this matter, came to the conclusion that *all* the gods had once been famous rulers. This theory came to be named "euhemerism" after him. This theory does not fit every god, but does explain the origin of a fair number of them. Others are accounted for by the attempt to personify natural processes.[12]

It has long been known that the worship of Jove, at least, spread much farther than the worship of a merely local deity.

The original Creator-God of the Aryans was known among all the Indo-European nations. His first name was *Dyaus Pitar* ('Divine Father') which is the same as the

Greek *Zeus Pater,* the Latin *Jupiter* or *Deus,* the early German *Tiu* or *Ziu,* and Norse *Tyr.* Another name was 'The Heavenly One' (Sanskrit *Varuna,* Greek *Ouranos*), or 'The Friend' (Sanskrit *Mitra,* Persian *Mithra*).[13]

When you collect all the versions of Jove and stick them together, you begin to see just how uninventive pagans really are. Jove bears a strong resemblance to the nastier type of modern tycoon, somewhat like J. R. Ewing in the TV show "Dallas," right down to his cheatin' heart. No wonder none of his followers wanted to meet the god they had created.

No Love of the Gods

It was no fun to meet a god. In fact, much of Greek religion was designed to *prevent* or at least mitigate the evils of such meetings.

In Homer's poems, no hero confessed to elation when a god revealed his presence. The hero did not court the gods or strive to meet them. He chanced upon them, and as the first terror left him, he might beg for practical, earthly favors. It took a very special hero, a child of one of the gods, to dare to protest to a god face to face. Other heroes were more restrained, and mere mortals, naturally, would observe the greatest restraint. . . . The experience of emotional warmth and reassurance and a sense of unity with surrounding nature were not the hallmarks of an encounter with a present divinity in early Greece.[14]

Syncretism

The Greeks loved to hear new things and follow new religions. Greek religion soon resembled the New Age rack in your local bookstore in the way it lumped together all kinds of pagan spirituality. Whereas the Pharisees of Jesus' time would travel over land and sea to gain a single proselyte, the Greeks would travel over land and sea to bring home a single strange new teaching.

> Greek magic has been influenced from time immemorial by Oriental beliefs. No nation welcomed foreign ideologies more warmly than the Hellenes. Priests, philosophers and historians roamed foreign lands. The quest for knowledge led the wonder-worker Apollonius of Tyana to the shores of India. Plato tells of cultural ties with Egypt and Crete. Greeks accompanied the Persians Darius and Xerxes on their expeditions. . . . Mythical figures and gods of the Orient have been hellenized. The Delphic cult originated in Crete; Adonis sprang from the Hebrew Adonai; Aphrodite is the embellished and pacified Astarte; Isis became Athene; and Dionysus hardly veils his alien origin.[15]

The only religion the Greeks refused to borrow from was Judaism. Although they had quite a bit of contact with the land of Palestine, the Greeks were simply too proud to believe such a simple and morally demanding doctrine as that of the God of Israel. It left no room for their love of technique and ritual. It gave the poor as much access to God as the rich, and the simple as much chance of spiritual enlightenment as the wise. Worst of all, the Israelites had a moral law that did *not* endorse all the Greeks' favorite kinds of sexual diversions.

No Sin

The idea of sin as an offense against a holy God and as involving guilt was almost wholly absent among the Greeks. Sin was conceived of rather as "ignorance, as a failure to understand. . . ."[16] The Greeks thus had holy *places*, but no holy *men*.[17] Their morals, such as they were, were "derived from human nature rather than from the being and mind of God."[18] Anyone who understands human nature realizes what an absolute mother lode of degeneracy this idea opens up.

Moral Egalitarianism

The Greeks considered themselves very wise and had a horror of "simplistic" teachings. This led them to tolerate everything *except* the belief that there was an obvious right and wrong in doctrine or practice. For, as Robin Lane Fox points out:

> If the Supreme God was unknowable, who was to say which one of the many cults of different peoples was right or wrong? At its heart, therefore, pagan theology could extend a peaceful coexistence to any worship which, in turn, was willing to coexist in peace. . . . In pagan "religiousness" there was no fear of heresy, no urge to orthodoxy and clerical "control." . . . Pagans' religious fear was a fear of the random anger of gods. . . .[19]

"Aphrodite Made Me Do It"

How can there be no right and wrong? Because the gods move you to do wrong just as often as they move you to do right. Among the Greeks, "Aphrodite made me do it" was a legitimate excuse for any sexual outrage.

> Aphrodite "puts desire" into animals [according to the *Homeric Hymn to Aphrodite*] as well as into men and gods. She leads astray "even the reason of Zeus"; it is she who "easily makes him mate with mortal wor en, unknown to

Hera." . . . By emphasizing the irreducible and irrational character of concupiscence, the *Hymn* justifies the amorous adventures of Zeus (which will, furthermore, be indefinitely repeated by gods, heroes, and men). In short, there is here a *religious* justification of [illegitimate] sexuality; for, incited by Aphrodite, even sexual excesses and outrages must be recognized as of divine origin.[20]

Similarly, acts of brutal violence could be blamed on the inspiration of the god Mars, acts of thievery on Hermes (the patron god of thieves), and so on. The only sins that counted were offenses against the gods themselves. As long as it was OK with the gods, it couldn't be wrong.

Perverted Heroes

As it turned out, almost everything was OK with the gods. The heroes, beloved of the gods, and whom moderns tend to think of as genuinely heroic, often acted more like Freddy from *Nightmare on Elm Street*. The real Greek myths were definitely not bedtime stories for little children. Together, the heroes perpetrated just about every disgusting deed the human mind has ever invented.

Classical Greece, and especially the Hellenistic period, left us a "sublime" vision of the heroes. In reality their nature is exceptional and ambivalent, even aberrant. The heroes prove to be at once good and bad and accumulate contradictory attributes. . . . They are distinguished by their strength and beauty but also by monstrous characteristics. . . . They are androgynous (Cecrops), or change their sex (Teiresias), or dress like women (Heracles). In addition, the heroes are characterized by numerous anomalies (acephaly or polycephaly; Heracles has three rows of teeth); they are apt to be lame, one-eyed, or blind. Heroes often fall victim to insanity (Orestes, Bellerophon, even the exceptional Heracles, when he slaughtered his sons . . .). As for their sexual behavior, it is excessive or abhorrent: Heracles impregnates the fifty daughters of Thespius in one night; Theseus is famous for his numerous rapes (Helen, Ariadne, etc.); Achilles ravishes Statonice. The heroes commit incest with their daughters or their mothers and indulge in massacres from envy or anger or often for no reason at all: they even slaughter their fathers and mothers or their relatives.[21]

Superstition

Early Greek life was an absolute mass of superstitions and fearful attempts to placate the gods. Only later, when philosophical schools such as the Epicureans and Stoics began to challenge the existence of the gods, did a few upper-class Greeks begin to shake free of a lifestyle bound by hundreds of complicated rituals and taboos.

Classical Greek writer Theophrastus gives us a picture of the life of the average Greek pagan in his work *The Characters.*

Obviously, superstitiousness would be generally defined as a kind of cowardice when confronted with the supernatural. The superstitious man is the sort of person who won't go out for the day without washing his hands and aspersing himself at the Nine Springs, and putting a piece of laurel-leaf from a temple in his mouth. If a cat runs across the road, he won't go any further until either someone else passes or he has thrown three stones across the road. If he sees a snake in his house, he calls on Sabazius, if it is one of the red variety; if it's one of the sacred sort, he builds a shrine on the spot. When he passes one of those smooth stones which stand at cross-roads, he pours a little oil from his flask over it, and won't go on till he has knelt down and bowed his head to the ground. . . . He is always ceremonially purifying his house . . . If he hears an owl hoot while he's out walking, he is much shaken and won't go past without muttering, "All power is Athene's." He refuses to set foot on a tombstone or go anywhere near a dead body or a woman in childbirth, saying he doesn't want to suffer pollution.

Every month on the fourth and seventh he gives instructions for wine to be mulled for his family; he goes out and buys myrtle-boughs, incense, and holy pictures, comes in again and spends the whole day making garlands for the hermaphrodites and offering them sacrifices. Every time he has a dream he rushes to the dream-experts, prophets, or augurs to inquire what god or goddess he ought to appease. . . .[22]

Even a pagan like Theophrastus can see that such behavior is ridiculous. Yet modern New Agers are feverishly attempting to discover all such ancient superstitions so they can *copy* them! It is only a step from a fun ritual that is supposed to get you extra power to a ritual you don't dare omit for fear of losing your place in the universe.

Fearful Magic

Not that the Greek philosophers really managed to evade the grip of magic and ritual. And please note, in ancient Greek religion, magic was used to *protect* yourself from the evil spiritual world, not as a way to put an extra tiger in your spiritual tank. *All* the ancient magical teachings stress the omnipresence of evil; only today are people foolish enough to believe in great spiritual powers without considering the possibility that some of them *must* be evil.

All the philosophers of old believed in the reality of magic. Heraclitus, Thales, Pindar, Xenophon, Socrates were unable to elude the enchanted circle. The later Greek philosophers, like Porphyry (A.D. 233-303), were entirely devoted to magical practices. . . . For Porphyry there existed innumerable beastly demons who haunted men and houses in their hankering after blood and filth. At meal times the demons swarm around us like flies, and only a complicated ritual can keep them away. These ceremonies were initiated not to please the gods but solely to repel devils.[23]

Miserable Life After Death

Life after death for the pagan Greeks was an unmitigated disaster. This probably goes far to explain why they were so intent on draining the cup of pleasure while on earth. Although they did not believe they would have to suffer through endless existences on earth, as did the Hindu Aryans, the Greek afterlife was a dreary, hopeless place resembling the Sheol of the Bible, from which their gods were unable to save them.

For Homer's contemporaries death was a diminished and humiliating postexistence in the underground darkness of Hades, peopled by pallid shadows, without strength and without memory. (Achilles, whose ghost Ulysses succeeds in calling up, declares that he would choose to be on earth the slave of a poor man, "rather than to reign over all the dead.")[24]

Whose God Is Too Small?

The main appeal of the Greek gods remains their indulgence of human sin. Aside from this trait, so appealing to the worst in human nature, they have nothing at all to recommend them. The gods are capricious, unlovable, even downright nasty specimens. They wield their power rather like a three-year-old might wield a blowtorch, scorching everyone around. They cannot save their followers in this life or the next.

All this does not stop modern pagans from trying to make the Greek gods sound bigger and nobler than the Christian God. One such writer, John Holland Smith, at the close of his book *The Death of Classical Paganism*, has the effrontery to say, "But the gods remain. And what they say is: your god is too small; there is divinity in things that his followers have ignored and decried; above all, there is divinity in generosity and acceptance of difference, though none in narrowness and exclusivity."[25] With this we contrast Robin Lane Fox's observation that, "The [pagan] gods came in pocket-sized models, so that anyone could travel with them and keep them handy."[26]

Now, really, *whose* god is too small?

Judgment on Greece

Greece, like every other pagan empire before it, was destined for a plot in of the graveyard of history. Even while Israel languished under the iron rule of Babylon, the prophet Daniel predicted that Greece would rise to world power under Alexander the Great — and subsequently be divided, diminished, and finally overthrown.[27] This prophecy was fulfilled to the letter.

Greece's influence, however, lingered long after its fall from power. In fact, Rome drew heavily from Greek ideas and culture. It wasn't until the downfall of Rome that pagan Greece was fully submerged.

The Greeks produced great beauty in what they produced, but their worship of beauty led to exposing newborns to death. Unbridled lust for beauty has its own casualties — the unlovely, deformed, and imperfect.

Their desire for order in society would have been

admirable if it had not been divorced from the *value of the individual in God's eyes.* Purely, utilitarian attempts at order destroy God's order.

Science, correctly used, reveals God's wisdom in creation and leads to His praise. But science that ignores God's existence and seeks to justify human endeavors and motives becomes a monstrous machine. Rationalism without faith is deadly — and as dead as the gods of Greece.

CHAPTER 10

ROME: CHRISTIANS AND PAGANS TAKE OFF THE GLOVES

After you, [O Nebuchadnezzar,] another kingdom will rise, inferior to yours. Next, a third kingdom, one of bronze, will rule over the whole earth. Finally, there will be a fourth kingdom, strong as iron — for iron breaks and smashes everything — and as iron breaks things to pieces, so it will crush and break all the others. . . .

In the time of those kings, the God of heaven will set up a kingdom that will never be destroyed, nor will it be left to another people. It will crush all those kingdoms and bring them to an end, but it will itself endure forever.

—Daniel 2:39, 40, 44

"**H**i! I'm Jove, and I'm here to conquer you." Or, as Julius Caesar put it, "I came, I saw, you're history."

This proud empire, one of the greatest in world history, was the first to bow the knee before the name of Jesus Christ. Pagan laws and practices were exchanged for Christian laws and practices. Emperors gave their fond approval — and often their money — to church efforts in evangelism and relief work. Everything from art to zoology was affected by the coming with power of the gospel of Christ.

Roman religion was very like Greek religion, so we don't need to look at it separately in any detail. It shared the same New Age emphasis on diversity and tolerance, the same interest in astrology and divination, and even the same Greek gods (with Baal, now known as Saturn, and a few other Mesopotamian gods thrown in).[1] The Romans were at first cooler than the Greeks about their religions, more interested in precisely following the correct rituals than in emotional highs, but ecstatic mystery cults became trendy during the first centuries A.D. for those who sought a religious jolt. The Romans were also extremely concerned that religion serve the ends of the godlike State. They were aware of the danger an unapproved cult could bring to their regimented society. Worldly-wise Rome was an unlikely candidate to be taken by surprise by a new religion.

Today Christians often expect the gospel to triumph only in unsophisticated areas, while expecting to continue to lose ground in highly developed cultures. Yet Rome had wealth and sophistication to burn. Two thousand years ago, wealthy

Romans had indoor plumbing, and some of the roads and bridges Romans built endure to this day. Roman trade encompassed the civilized world and beyond, and Roman management skills allowed Rome to rule over provinces separated by thousands of miles. Furthermore, Rome was a thoroughly pagan society to begin with, one proud of its traditions. Pagans controlled the arts, the sports, the government, and the bureaucracy. Whole industries were built on supporting the pagan traditions, such as the craftsmen who made statues of the gods.

Against this might of pagan Rome were pitted a few hundred disciples of a Jewish carpenter named Jesus. Soon it would be legal to inform on them and to kill them in the gladiatorial ring. Governors would be required to ferret out the Christians and destroy them. Pagan priests would whip their followers into frenzies of Christian-bashing, blaming every disaster from bad weather to a barbarian uprising on the Christians. Under such conditions, most of the new Christians would have no social standing. Few wise, wealthy, or influential people would join them. The church, with its commitment to care for the poor, would find itself mostly made up of the poor, the dregs of Roman society. In Las Vegas, the odds would easily have been a thousand to one against the Christians.

All the same, the Christians won.

Now, how exactly did this happen?

The Blood of the Martyrs Is the Blood of the Martyrs

Sentimentalists like to quote Tertullian's phrase, "The blood of the martyrs is the seed of the church," as an explanation for how the ragtag band of Christians managed to grow, thrive, and take over the Empire. This is absolutely incorrect. The blood of the martyrs is not and never has been the seed of the church. More often, it is the death of the church. The Christian church in Japan was effectively wiped out for four centuries by the massacre of Japanese Christians starting in 1597. The Protestant church in Spain was successfully destroyed by the Spanish Inquisition. The St. Bartholomew's Day Massacre in pre-revolutionary France was the beginning of the end for French Protestantism (and, some think, for French Catholicism as well).

The massacre of Christians is not guaranteed to produce more Christians. In fact, to call the martyrs' blood "the seed of the church," as if there were some cause-and-effect relationship between martyrdoms and church growth, actually *dishonors* God by detracting from the miracle of church growth occurring *in spite of* martyrdoms. It is as if we said, "Being thrown into the fire is the seed of emerging unscathed from the fire." Yes, God delivered Shadrach, Meshach, and Abednego out of the fiery furnace . . . but it was a *miracle*, not the result of some natural law!

There are some among us today who talk as if a great wave of physical persecution would be the best thing for the church today. Consider. Do you think that being forbidden to evangelize upon pain of imprisonment, or forbidden to train your children as Christians upon threat of having them removed from your custody into a state institution, would be a blessing for church growth? Would being forbidden to gather in groups facilitate Christian training? Would laws rewarding informers with the property of condemned Christians help spur a revival? Anyone who thinks so is free to emigrate to the Worker's Paradise of Soviet Russia where all this, and much more, awaits the earnest seeker after martyrdom.

No. All this loose talk about the benefits of martyrs' blood simply sidesteps the *real* reasons for how Christians took over the Roman Empire. Christians today are not under some strange disadvantage because of the shortage of lions longing to eat us. We can find out, and put into practice, the same strategies that delivered Rome into the Christian camp.

Christ versus Caesar

But first, what exactly were the pagan Romans and the born-again Christians contending about? We today tend to think that they were arguing over which religion was true—Christianity or paganism. In a sense this was correct. That was the real issue. But Christians were not thrown to the lions for believing in Jesus. In Rome, you could believe in Jesus, or Mithra, or Isis, or Jahweh, or any god or combination of gods, without fear of reprisals. Christians were thrown to the lions for believing that *Jesus is Lord*.

Rome, you see, had religious freedom—of a sort. You could believe anything you wanted to as long as you upheld the right of other people to believe anything *they* wanted to, and as long as you acknowledged Caesar as a god.

Why did the early Christians die rather than offer a pinch of incense before a statue of Caesar? We all know the answer from Sunday school. They would worship no god but the Christian Trinity. That is fairly obvious and simple. What is not so obvious and simple is *why the Roman government insisted that the Christians sacrifice to Caesar*. What did they care who Christians worshiped? What did it matter to them?

The answer is tremendously important for us today. Roman leaders did not want Christians "imposing their morality" on *them*. For Caesar to be god meant that Caesar made the laws; he could not be judged by any "higher" law. Christians believed in a higher law by which *all men,* including rulers, were to be judged. This struck at the very heart of the Roman secular state.

This belief in the absolute right of the leader to do whatever he wants is the essential underpinning of every tyranny that has ever existed on the face of the earth. No tyrant can afford to acknowledge the existence of a higher lord than himself, to whose laws he is accountable.

The early Christian leaders knew this. That is why the first recorded prayer of the apostles in the Book of Acts was for boldness to speak out for Jesus *in spite of* the opposition of the civil rulers (Acts 4:24-31). In this prayer, the apostles quoted Psalm 2:1, 2:

> *Why do the nations rage*
> *and the peoples plot in vain?*
> *The kings of the earth take their stand*
> *and the rulers gather together*
> *against the Lord*
> *and against his Anointed One.*

The next verse of the Psalm goes on to explain why the rulers are so angry with the Trinity. "'Let us break their chains,' they say, 'and throw off their fetters.'" Pagan rulers *hate* God's absolute laws. They want to be gods and make their own laws, without any restraints on them at all!

Bible history is the story of God's men confronting rulers with the message that rulers cannot just do whatever they like. Think of the prophet Nathan telling off David for his adultery, and of the constant stream of prophets who confronted the kings and leaders of both Israel and Judah. Think of Daniel warning Nebuchadnezzar to repent of his evil deeds, and how God subsequently humbled Nebuchadnezzar in order to impress this message on him. Remember how John the Baptist met his end as a result of telling King Herod it was not right for him to have his brother's wife? We could multiply examples. Suffice it to say that recognizing Jesus as the "King of Kings" means that rulers, as well as their people, are called to bow the knee before Him. The Christian message was that the law was *not* just whatever Caesar said it was, just as today the message must be that the law is *not* just whatever the Supreme Court says it is.

This might appear to be a dangerous mission, and it is. However, God can use even "the wrath of man" to praise Him (Psalm 76:10).

Strangely, the very success of first Greek, then Roman totalitarianism helped prepare the way for the gospel.

Greece provided a universal language known throughout the Roman Empire. . . . It also provided the pagan conceptual frameworks of Greek philosophy. . . .

The Romans provided stable government, a system of roads superior to any before it, and the Pax Romana. The latter meant that travel around the Roman Empire was safe. . . .[2]

Of course, these same advantages of easy travel and a universal language applied to all of the hundreds of Roman cults, not just to Christianity. But Christianity was different in a number of important ways from the gaggle of approved religions.

Certainty of Truth and Intolerance of Error

Today, as in Roman times, waffling is in. Christians "dialog" about all sorts of previously non-negotiable issues. Church councils meet to debate the advisability of female elders and homosexual marriage. Pundits ponder *which* parts of the Bible are truth, while feminists take an X-acto knife to Bible history ("the record of patriarchal bias") and doctrinal teaching ("Our Mother, who art in Heaven").

This kind of religious tolerance was well known in the first centuries after Christ — among pagans.

Never was there a more tolerant age than that into which Christianity appeared. . . .Syncretism was the religious hall-mark of the time. . . . There was no clear line of demarcation among the foreign cults, which showed a marked hospitality in religion. Different gods agreed to be housed in the same temple; the same priest might officiate for half a dozen deities. Men were willing to try every religion and philosophy in the field. It was now as fashionable to owe allegiance to the gods of the Nile, Syria, Persia, Samothrace, Greece, and Rome, as it had been in the previous

epoch to acknowledge only one national pantheon. Polytheism is naturally tolerant, and the spirit of the Age only
increased religious tolerance. . . .[3]

The Christians did not share in this feel-good spirit of universal tolerance. Christians had *truth,* and were not in a mood
to trade it for the supposed "insights" of pagans. While
pagans patted each other on the back and affirmed each
other's self-worth, Christian preachers talked of sin and a
judgment to come. The New Testament epistles strongly
denounced error and warned church leaders to bounce out
the heretics who were bound to sneak in. God Himself took a
hand in enforcing church discipline — witness the sudden
deaths of Ananias and Sapphira,[4] and the judgments threatened against the false prophetess Jezebel.[5] The areas for tolerance and genuine disagreement were spelled out — matters of
which days to celebrate unto the Lord, of what kind of food
and drink to consume. The nature of Christ, the necessity of
repentance, the roles of men and women, and sexual morality
— among other things — were not negotiable.

Christianity, unlike the pagan cults based on myths, was
a historical religion. The early Christians knew that Jesus
had actually lived, died, and been resurrected. Instead of sit-
ting around picking at the Gospels trying to locate the "historical Jesus," they *knew* the historical Jesus. The earliest
Christians had seen Christ in person; those who came later
not only had a personal relationship with Christ in their spirits, but had the documents of Matthew, Mark, Luke, and
John to consult.

Where the Bacchic societies offered a myth of their god,
Jews and Christians offered history; the pagan mysteries
conveyed a secret experience, whereas the Jews and Christians offered a "revelation" based on texts.[6]

The Christians . . . could cite prophecies . . . they knew
exactly who God was, in an age of discreet uncertainty;

their God was a God of history, proven in events; after all, he had sent a Son, to redeem men by actions of total selflessness.[7]

This Christian certainty spilled over to matters of morals and philosophy. Pagans tried, and failed, to reason out answers about the origin of the world and the proper conduct of human beings; Christians *knew* the answers. They were written down in God's book, the Bible. And, unlike pagan teachings, the Bible was not subject to change. Anyone who added to or took away from the canonical writings would come under mighty judgment. The Bible itself said so.

> The Christians . . . united ritual and philosophy and brought the certainty of God and history to questions whose answers eluded the pagan schools.[8]

This *intolerance* preserved the fledgling Church from the wasting disease of syncretism with which the Roman Empire languished. In seeking to make the gate wide and the road broad that led to religious acceptance, the Roman cults succeeded only into finally blending together and losing their collective credibility.

> In the matter of intolerance Christianity differed from all pagan religions, and surpassed Judaism; in that respect it stood in direct opposition to the spirit of the age. . . .
>
> But we shall less regret this intolerance of primitive Christianity when we reflect upon the nature and necessity of it. . . . Tolerance too often results from indifference or indecision, but the intolerance of the Christian preachers was that of the conviction that they had found *the* all-comprehensive Truth. And in the welter of religions and philosophies intolerance was the most obvious, if not also the only sure, method of self-preservation. . . . The hospitality and syncretism of the competitors of Christianity,

while greatly adding to their popularity, ultimately compassed their downfall.[9]

People did not join the church in order to experience warm fellowship, get a religious high, reach their full potential, or solve their psychological problems. They joined because the Christian message was *true*.

Boldness

The first recorded prayer of the apostles after Christ's return to Heaven was a prayer for boldness in confronting the Jewish and pagan authorities (Acts 4:24–30). The first Christians knew the world was not prepared to welcome them with open arms. However, instead of bemoaning the evilness of those "end times" and using their obvious weakness as an excuse for inaction, they got busy attacking spiritual strongholds.

The funny thing was that it *worked!*

It must have come as a surprise to the vigilant Roman authorities to discover that a new religion, with apparently no past, should suddenly appear upon the stage professing to be a universal religion and disputing the imperial cult. . . . Christianity waxed stronger while opposed by the State, by other popular religions, by its parent faith, by the science and philosophies of the time.[10]

Christians of that time did not believe in presenting Christian claims in religiously neutral terms. Their leaders would tell anyone from the meanest slave to the emperor himself that certain things were right and certain things were wrong *because God had declared them right or wrong*. They were not ashamed to speak of sin and repentance, Heaven and Hell. It did not occur to them to protect the crowds' fragile self-worth; when Peter had an opportunity to preach to his fellow Jews in Jerusalem he told them straight out that they were accessories in crucifying Christ.[11] This kind of preaching brought results: sometimes stonings and beatings, but also deep and lasting conversions.

Selflessness

In contrast with both today's and yesterday's New Age emphasis on, "What can the gods do for me?" Christians asked their Lord, "What can I do for You?" And those, whether rich or poor, who performed notable service for their fellowmen were honored by the church as an example for others to follow.

In looking over the stories of early Christian saints, it is fascinating to see what a diverse bunch they are. Some are rich, some are poor. Some are old, some are young. Some are beautiful, some are homely. Some are slave, some are free. Some are Jewish, some are Gentile. Some are male, some are female. Some are married, some are virgins. None of them were honored for their image — dressing for success was more likely to disqualify a candidate for sainthood than enhance his or her chances. Most of them would not be honored, or even treated respectfully, if they attended many churches today. We seem to have room for only one Mother Teresa. But the ancient church had *thousands*.

> The cults and myths gave pagans a focus for their "feverish civic patriotism," yet Christians obeyed one law, the same from city to city.... At their festivals, the great pagan families made distributions to the small class of councillors, to the male citizens and lastly, if at all, to their women. Christians brought their funds to those in need, men and women, citizen and non-citizen. . . . The idea of "doing unto others as you would wish them to do unto you" was not foreign to pagan ethics, but there was no precedent for the further Christian advice to "love one's enemies." At its

best, such selflessness has always been its best argument. . . .[12]

Bill Pride has written a book, *Flirting with the Devil* (Crossway Books, 1988), in which he points out, among other things, why and how the church today actually discourages saintliness by an overpreoccupation with not making the unsaintly feel bad. The New Testament church had no such preoccupation. Christian leaders of that day were anxious to hold up every good example they could find in order to spur the others on to more good works. Instead of spending its efforts on trying to "cure" sins, the church put its weight behind getting people to work doing good deeds.

Humility

Pride was the hallmark of the pagan cults, as it is the hallmark of paganism today. "You shall be like God" was the original temptation in the Garden of Eden, and early Christians avoided it like the plague.

The ideal Christian did not push, did not shove, did not boast, did not consider himself above other people or above humble duties. He also did not spend long hours, or even long minutes, thinking about how wonderful he was or trying to think of himself as wonderful. Untoward behavior was not attributed to poor self-esteem — Christians were not supposed to have any self-esteem at all. Loving oneself was not only low on the priority list, it was off the list entirely. Loving others and loving God was what counted. The ideal was provided by Jesus Christ, who had turned His back on His own needs and desires for the sake of His mission to save His people.

All this totally flummoxed the pagans. How could Christians be so dead to a sense of their own honor, their own worth? How could they bear to turn the other cheek, go the extra mile, serve the ungracious, and love their enemies?

Everyone knew that humility was the mark of slaves and the degraded poor. Pagans saw no point in it; it disgusted them.

> Among pagan authors, "humility" had almost never been a term of commendation. Men were born "sons of God," said the Stoics, and thus they should cherish no "humble or ignoble" thoughts about their nature. The humble belonged with the abject, the mean, the unworthy. Christianity, however, ascribed humility to God's own Son and exalted it as a virtue of man.[13]

The pagans would have understood the humble Christians better if they had known Jesus' saying that the meek would inherit the earth. . . .

Hope

Perhaps the biggest differences between the New Testament church and the modern church are in the area of hope and vision.

When Christians today talk of world evangelism, they do so in terms of winning a few souls out of every tribe and nation, not in terms of Christian victory over the tribes and nations. The hope of many is to be raptured out of the earth, not to be found faithfully *working* when Jesus comes. The real gains Christians of the past made in establishing Christ's Lordship in education, laws, medicine, and so on are treated like accidents and ignored, rather than held up as examples to inspire us.

For several generations we have been told to expect total defeat in this world. The result has been apathy and a disinclination to leave the cozy Christian fortress, which is rapidly becoming less cozy as its territory radically diminishes.

Such thinking was totally foreign to the early Christians.

Their [the Jews' and Christians'] converts, we have seen, were not abandoning a static or dying [pagan] religious culture. Rather, they were joining the most extreme option in a period when religious issues were very lively; their chosen option joined cult and philosophy; it gave a clear code of conduct; it promised hope and an absolute triumph over death and Fate. [14]

People are willing to deny themselves and perform heroic feats if they are working to fulfill a vision they believe in. During wartime men willingly subject themselves to miserable living conditions, poor or nonexistent food, and the prospect of imminent and painful death, in order to win the victory for their side.

The New Testament church shared this militant spirit. They remembered the prophecy in Daniel that "a rock cut out, but not by human hands" would grow to fill the whole earth, and they knew that this "rock" was the church.[15] They had a mission; they intended to fulfill it; and they did fulfill it. All the might of New Age religion, backed up by the full power of the State, was unable to prevent a Christian takeover of pagan Rome.

PART 3

THE CHRISTIAN AGE

CHAPTER 11

PAGANISM A.D.

There will be terrible times in the last days. People will be lovers of themselves, lovers of money, boastful, proud, abusive, disobedient to their parents, ungrateful, unholy, without love, unforgiving, slanderous, without self-control, brutal, not lovers of the good, treacherous, rash, conceited, lovers of pleasure rather than lovers of God. . . . But they will not get very far because . . . their folly will be clear to everyone.

—2 Timothy 3:1–4, 9

S o far we have been concerned to prove that the New Age is not new. Now we are about to prove something even more important — that the New Age has *always* been with us.

Christian books on the New Age often make it sound as if the New Age is an absolutely unprecedented phenomenon, and as if its arrival must be proof that this is The End.

The truth, however, is that ever since the Montanists (a Phrygian cult) proclaimed they were bringing in a New Age in A.D. 160,[1] New Agers have been a dime a dozen. Even before then the Christian church was cursed with an influx of gnostics, who honored the idea of elite, "hidden" revelation. And in all times and all places, everywhere the church displaced paganism, a few were found who tried to hang on to the pagan traditions of their ancestors.

The real difference between now and then is not the *presence* of New Age teaching, but the *openness* of New Age teaching. While New Agers of the past were usually careful to stay underground, today's New Agers appear on national TV. This indeed is a sign of some importance, but it does not necessarily point to the imminent demise (or even rapture) of the church, as we will see.

We are now going to put on our hunting boots and follow the uneven progress of underground paganism in the Western world. We will find why the New Age has broken from cover, and why it was never able to do so successfully before.

Missionaries Sweep Away the New Age

The history of Christian missions throws much light onto the current conflict between Christians and New Agers. Throughout the church age, missionaries have gone into totally pagan regions and seen the pagans convert to Christianity. For all but the most modern, liberal missionaries this also meant sweeping changes in the formerly pagan cultures.

When Gregory the Enlightener, Christian missionary to Armenia in the late third and early fourth century, succeeded in converting the Armenians' king, he leveled the temple of the goddess Anahit, rather than preserving it as an "important cultural artifact." Boniface, "the Apostle of Germany," chopped down the sacred oak of Thor at Giesmar in Hesse, thus proving that Thor could not even defend his own tree. The Germans were instantly convinced that the God of Boniface really was stronger, and let him take the wood to build a chapel in honor of St. Peter! One of the first things St. Gall did when he arrived in northeastern Switzerland was to level the local pagan sanctuary. Even Gregory the Great, the accommodating bishop of Rome, admitted that, although pagan temples could sometimes be turned into Christian churches and pagan festivals into Christian holy days, the idols and pagan rituals had to go.

For the early missionaries, there was no such thing as religious neutrality. Cultural practices were either Christian or pagan. Christians buried their dead; pagans burned them (often accompanied by their wives and servants). Christians married one wife for life; pagans had wives, concubines, and sometimes boys and beasts as well. Pagans got drunk; Christians stayed sober. Even one's dress or the way a field was plowed could reflect pagan beliefs about honoring the gods — and if so, they would have to be changed.

Wherever missionaries had the chance, they wheedled, persuaded, or even forced their converts to replace pagan laws, ceremonies, sexual practices, business practices, and so on with what they considered the proper Christian way to do things. For this they have incurred the supercilious scorn of modern Western historians, who tend to ignore the difficulties of allowing total freedom of religion to people who sincerely believe in infant sacrifice and child prostitution.

While the memory of paganism was green, Christians were in no hurry to allow it back in. So the remaining pagans went underground, conducting their rituals with much secrecy in the dead of night. If caught, they were subjected to severe penalties.

Eventually, paganism as a religion died out in most Christian lands, to the point where we today don't even know why Stonehenge (for example) was built or what rituals went on there. Pagan influence only remained in superstitious folk practices and the pervasive tales of trolls, goblins, imps, and fairies — all types of spirits feared by the pagan ancestors. Even the fairy stories, though, now featured trolls scared away by the sound of church bells or the sight of the Cross.

Are Witches Pagans?

At one time it was thought that witchcraft was the remnant of an old pagan religion. The *New Encyclopedia Britannica* tries to scotch that notion:

> These [modern] so-called witches claim to be adherents of an ancient religion, the one to which Christianity is regarded as a counter-religion, and in this way they seek to secure public recognition of their eccentric activities by appealing to the cherished modern value of religious toleration.
>
> [Modern witches] usually turn out to be entirely sincere but misguided people who have been directly or indirectly influenced by Margaret Murray's article "Witchcraft," pub-

lished in the 14th edition of *Encyclopedia Britannica* (1929), which put forth in its most popular form her theory that the witches of western Europe were the lingering adherents of a once general pagan religion that has been displaced, though not completely, by Christianity. This highly imaginative but now discredited theory gave a new respectability to witchcraft and, along with the more practical influence of such modern practitioners as Aleister Crowley and Gerald Gardner, contributed to the emergence of self-styled witches that are sometimes featured in the sensationalist press.[2]

We think it is probable that modern Satanism is the child of medieval witchcraft, which itself is the leftover of all the worst parts of ancient religions.[3] The witches did not invent human sacrifice or perverse sexual rituals, after all; these go back to the ancient empire of Babylonia. Pure naked devil-worship, however, is somewhat unusual in ancient religion. Generally, the ancient peoples were aiming for some benefit — good crops, victory in battle — not just trying to throw the most evil party they could. Christianity provides plenty of means for praying for such things, though, and it had been proved to be the stronger religion. The only reason for hanging on to old-fashioned paganism was because you enjoyed the blood and sex. This theory would adequately explain both the presence of witches and their lack of the better features of ancient pagans.

But medieval witches were not the only pagan force Christians had to contend with. More significant were the secret societies. These started as individuals interested in the practice of "white" magic.[4] In their own way, they considered themselves scientists, searching out the spiritual laws that would enable them to perform wonders.

Most numerous were the alchemists, of whom Paracelsus was the most famous. Alchemy had its practical, materialist side. The alchemists were famous for their attempts to turn lead and other relatively worthless substances into gold. But allied with the practice of alchemy was the eternal desire for hidden knowledge and special powers, which since the Garden of Eden has always led to paganism.

Secret Societies

In time, alchemy had produced enough interest that an attempt was made to gather men of this frame of mind together.

> In 1614 there appeared a pamphlet written in German, entitled *The Reformation of the World*. . . . The brief satirical treatise used the god Apollo as spokesman, assisted by the wise men of antiquity and of the modern world, and proposed an attempt to reform the universe; or rather, it maintained that Apollo had made such an attempt in vain. . . . It appealed to many intelligent people of various countries and was reprinted and translated many times. It is safe to say that the originator of this text was an Italian, Trajano Boccalini, whose book had appeared two years earlier in Venice, and who was murdered in the following year. [T]he German version . . . contained in an addition a manifesto: *Fama Fraternitatis, or a Discovery of the Fraternity of the Most Laudable Order of the Rosy Cross.* [5]

This book recounted the mythical adventures of the Illuminated Father and Brother Christian Rosencrutz, as he toddled about the world obtaining secret wisdom from sages near and far. Once home, he spent his time studying and training his three disciples. The book ended with an affirmation that the Brothers were Christians and an appeal to others to join them — although the Brothers had neglected to tell who they were or where they might be found.

Kurt Seligman, author of *The History of Magic and the Occult*, says, "Ever since, secret societies have exerted their attraction upon men."[6] This is not terribly accurate, since the

Rosicrucians were just following in the footsteps of ancient mystery cults such as the early A.D. cults of Mithra and Isis. Note their appeal to *hidden wisdom* and their use of the god Apollo as spokesman for their cause.

Next on the scene were our old friends the Freemasons (today known simply as the Masonic Society). The Masons had been around since the eighth century or so, and you can find any number of books accusing them of plots to reestablish paganism in Christian countries. Be that as it may, the occult Rosicrucians formed the backbone of the new Masonic revival.

It was through [Valentine] Andrae [a Lutheran pastor who authored several treatises and books promoting Rosicrucianism] that Freemasonry, which probably originated in the eighth or ninth century, gained a new impetus. In 1645 a few English Rosicrucians met for the purpose of organizing their efforts. . . . They justified their secrecy with the claim that the general intolerance of that wicked epoch would not otherwise endure them, and they had to find ways of gaining new members despite their concealment. Elias Ashmole found the solution. As every Londoner was obliged by custom to be a member of a corporation, Ashmole registered himself as a stonemason; the others followed his example and under the sign of the masons they now met freely in the assembly hall of the corporation. From this group of Ashmoleans originated the ceremonial of the Freemasons.[7]

Freemasonry was not the friendly do-good organization that its modern followers claim it is. Christians of that day already had hundreds of monasteries, nunneries, charitable orders, and so on they could join if they wanted to help their fellow man. Rather, the Freemasons' root interest was in reviving pagan teachings.

The Freemasons and especially the Martinists, shared the ancient ideal of raising man from sin to felicity. Initiatory

rites were reminiscent of paganism. The candidates'
ordeal was inspired by Greek and Egyptian precedents.
The Masons were to be regenerated, like the initiates of
Eleusis, to ascend to higher realms and thus acquire
knowledge, revelation, and secret wisdom.[8]

It didn't take the secret societies long to start working
against the settled order of things.

Opposition against the decaying organization of the state
was advocated and fostered by Freemasons, Martinists,
Rosicrucians and Swedenborgians with more or less
vigor. . . . For the most part the Brothers were peace-loving
citizens and the fear they inspired was greater than the
danger they actually embodied. Their resistance was pas-
sive — but it was resistance.
    The fear they inspired in the authorities soon led to the
persecution of the brotherhoods. Such a policy created
martyrs, heroes, opponents. In 1738 Pope Clement XII
excommunicated all the Freemasons of Europe; and Louis
XV interdicted Masonry in France.[9]

Louis XV was, as usual, too late. Not long after he outlawed Freemasonry, he lost his head at the guillotine.
    Other secret societies were the Martinists and the Swe-
denborgians.

The French occult connection in Haiti derives from two
eighteenth-century mystics, Louis Claude de Saint-Martin
and Martinez de Pasqually. The latter was a Rosicrucian
disciple of Amanuel Swedenborg, and the founder of an
occult group called the Order of the Elect Cohens. . . .
Saint-Martin joined de Pasqually's order in 1768 and after
the leader's death in 1774 became the dominant figure in
the group. Collectively they became known as Martinists.
There were Martinist orders in several different regions of
France . . . and by the end of the eighteenth century, also

167

in Haiti, [where] the tradition tended to blend with Voodoo.

After a period in abeyance, Martinism revived in Haiti in the 1890s and between the two world wars.[10]

Pasqually's Swedenborgian rites were modified by his friend Louis Claude de Saint-Martin (1743–1803) who spread the doctrine all over Europe. . . . The Martinists had their associates in Russia, especially among the nobles. . . . The great attraction exerted by the Martinists were magic rites which resemble those of modern spiritualists. The dead were evoked, and hallucinations were stimulated by magic circles, aromatic herbs, beautiful black silk robes and diamond-studded insignia.[11]

As you see, *magic* and *pagan gods* were extremely important to all these societies. They were *secret* societies, for the very good reason that the average man in the street was opposed to such heathen goings-on.

France Goes Pagan

Things began to change at the beginning of the eighteenth century, especially in France. The first mass introduction to paganism began, strangely, with the death of a Christian deacon.

In the first quarter of the eighteenth century a young man, the deacon François de Paris (1690–1727), a Jansenist, lived in the capital [Paris] in piety and seclusion. After his death strange events took place at his tomb in the St. Médard cemetery. . . .

St. Médard resembled a witches' sabbath. The aspect of the frenzied crowd, the display of hideous diseases, the howls and the macabre surroundings bore little resemblance to that elegance and refinement which we ordinarily associate with the eighteenth century. But these scenes were enhanced by the aura of the marvelous. [He then relates various miraculous cures that happened there.]

The disregard of the rigid, classic, Apollonian ideal, and the acceptance of the Dionysian frenzy, the uncontrolled, is significant in the epoch following the death of the dominating Louis XIV, who believed that he was the state and who called himself the Sun King (Apollo). . . .

[Once Jansenism and St. Médard were suppressed] the miraculous cures, however, now happened infrequently, and in their place developed a tendency towards self-torture. . . . Instead of healing, the saint now spread suffering. . . .[12]

While the happenings at St. Médard mostly interested the peasantry, the nobles also had their own version of pagan awakening. Fifty years after the outbreak at St. Médard, Paris was rocked by a gruesome scandal involving ranking members of the nobility. Highly born men and ladies had become involved with an infant-sacrifice cult run by a woman called Catherine La Voisin (which, ironically, means "The Neighbor").

La Voisin told fortunes with coffee grounds and a magical crystal; but this divinatory trade was only a façade for larger enterprises. She evoked the dead and the devil, and solemnized magical rites in her back-chambers. She had many assistants, among them the two hangmen of Paris who brought her horrible gifts from the gibbet. Abbé Guibourg, a priest of noble descent, then sixty years old, performed black masses. Madame de Montespan offered herself as 'altar cloth.' She lay naked on the altar; the chalice was placed upon her belly; Guibourg slit an infant's throat and let the blood run down into the chalice. Many other equally dreadful acts were committed. . . .

La Voisin was burned at the stake in 1680. Several who were indicted died in prison; others committed suicide.

Thirty-six were executed; five were sent to the galleys; one hundred and forty-seven were sentenced to prison. Among the indicted were the flower of the French nobility. . . . However, the nobility were spared. . . . To the counts and duchesses, the whole indictment seemed a bad joke. When the Councillor of State asked the Duchess of Bouillon whether she had seen the devil during those evocations, she answered, "I see him right now; he is disguised as a Councillor of State, and he looks rather ugly!" Everybody laughed. Yet during the black masses these witty people had witnessed the slaughter of two thousand five hundred babies.[13]

These pagan outbreaks coincided with the beginning of the so-called "Age of Reason," also known as the Enlightenment. As Kurt Seligman perceptively points out:

We have already gathered, from the happenings at St. Médard, that the so-called skeptical period ushered in by the eighteenth century was less skeptical than has been supposed. The number of occult publications did not diminish but rather increased. The old prophecies were revived and reprinted along with new ones for an expanding public. Secret societies found leaders and grew quickly. Magi and seers attracted public interest; magical cures, alchemy, divining rods, physiognomy, mystical sects, were the talk of the town. . . . Louis XV was fond of working in his alchemical laboratory; and the royal example encouraged many gentlemen at court, as well as the citizens of Paris. . . .

Ancient magical texts were systematically compiled.[14]

As students of history know, this new French fanaticism culminated in the bloody French Revolution. The revolutionaries dressed up an opera singer as the Goddess of Liberty and held worship services devoted to her. They outlawed every form of Christianity and even tried to abolish the seven-day week as established at Creation. Secret police roamed everywhere, accusing thousands of innocent people of plots against the godlike State. Before things settled down, France had experienced such horrors as had never before been seen in a Christian nation. All under the name of bringing in a New Age of Fraternity, Equality, and Liberty.

England Goes Christian

Across the Channel, Englishmen watched with horror as the French nation covered itself with blood. But England was destined not to experience such a bloodbath, even though the same factors that precipitated the French Revolution could be found in England. Although the English lower classes had been decimated by drunkenness and their social superiors looked upon them as subhuman beings, social frictions never erupted into open battle. The difference was that while France was giving itself over to paganism, England was experiencing a Christian revival.

England, too, had its secret societies. A group of young lords had named themselves the Hellfire Club and were engaged in evil pagan rituals. Masons and Martinists could be found in England as well as in France. But in England a small group of young Christian university students had been led by the Holy Spirit to attack spiritual strongholds. Titled the "Holy Club" by their detractors, and later called "Methodists," they refused to let lords or bishops, drunken thugs, or scornful philosophers slow them down. When they were denied the use of the churches, they preached in the fields. George Whitefield, the most accomplished preacher of the group, even ventured to take up his stand in the English equivalent of Times Square, preaching to the people gathered for amusement at Kennington Common.

Kennington Common was an area of about twenty acres and lay south of the Thames. It was especially notable as the scene of hangings. . . . If the habitués of Moorfields were rough, those of Kennington were brutal, for here the lowest of London's citizens congregated in teeming numbers. Here were vicious sports and drunken brawlings. Here the harlot and pick-pocket sought the victim of their trades, and here the mob assembled, ready for any act of violence. . . .

Moved with compassion . . . Whitefield walked out upon Kennington Common and proceeded to take the enemy's citadel by storm.[15]

Nor were Whitefield's colleagues, among whom were John and Charles Wesley and the indefatigable Welshman Howell Harris, any less courageous. They all were bold, certain of the truth of their message and intolerant of error, selfless, admirers of humility, lovers of holiness, and believed that God could do great things. These were not men to sit around bemoaning the evils of the times. They got up and went on the offensive, preaching the gospel to the dissolute nobility as well as to the degenerate coal miners, passionately urging them to change their practices as well as their beliefs. And this was in an age when any kind of religious fervor was labeled "enthusiasm" and the fashionable belief was to believe in nothing.

As a direct result of the Methodist revival, slavery was abolished in Britain (*without* a civil war); labor laws were changed to prevent factory owners from exploiting children and women; Sunday schools were started to teach the children of the poor Christian doctrine and how to read; the Gin Craze ended; the London mob disbanded; debtor's prison was abolished; pornography disappeared off the bookstands; mental hospitals were reformed; nursing societies were started; and the great missionary movement of the nineteenth century began.

Yet, at the same time as this mighty work of God was going forth, another movement was beginning to roll that would eventually, if not stopped, undo every bit of good the

revival had wrought. It did not appear to be a pagan movement on the surface, yet it has led directly to every New Age
book, video, TV show, public school class, law, medical practice, and so on that you have ever seen or ever will see. It can
be stopped; the Methodists in England challenged it head-on
as it was just beginning, and stopped it cold. But Christians
today, not recognizing it, have actually *encouraged* it to take
over our culture.

May God help us as we look in the next chapter at the
real power of the New Age in the world today.

CHAPTER 12

THE ENDARKENMENT STRIKES

When a strong man, fully armed, guards his own house, his possessions are safe. But when someone stronger attacks and overpowers him, he takes away the armor in which the man trusted and divides up the spoils.

He who is not with me is against me, and he who does not gather with me, scatters.

—Jesus Christ, in Luke 11:21-23

We have traced the obvious pagan strand in Western history until the eighteenth century: witches celebrating their black sabbaths in the forests of England, secret societies performing ancient Egyptian rituals, rich French noblemen worshiping Mother Astarte with the blood of Parisian babies. This strand, while not wholly negligible, had little effect on the lives of most people of the time. Now it's time to examine the movement that, at last, laid a successful foundation for a wholescale pagan revival in Christendom.

The Church Makes Some Mistakes

We start our journey at the age known as the Renaissance. It was a time of immense interest in the achievements of older civilizations. Scholars and antiquarians were uncovering almost daily new proof of the glories of Greece and Rome. Many, if not most, of these scholars were Christians interested in "spoiling the Egyptians" as the famous theologian Augustine, Bishop of Hippo, had suggested; in other words, they wanted to glean what knowledge and insight they could from the achievements of the ancients without becoming ensnared by pagan philosophy. They were hoping for a Christian Renaissance. Others, less wary, found themselves opening their hearts to the gods themselves. These latter had little immediate effect, however. John Holland Smith, author of *The Death of Classical Paganism*, a work which mourns the demise of paganism, says of the Renaissance:

Here at least was something: the skill and the art of those who had produced such treasures of literature and sculpture no longer lacked appreciation. Through recognition of their artistry, the gods were no longer mocked. But could they themselves ever return, to reign beside Christ, perhaps, if never to replace him? There were those who dreamed that they could, although no movement to revive them ever found favour except among small circles of (often unbalanced) intellectuals, cut off by their aspirations, their vocabulary, and usually by their affluence from the mass of the people around them.[1]

The printing presses were not idle, though. Soon after Gutenberg invented the process of printing with movable type, printers were making available "to scholars and people alike Greek and Roman classics that were steeped in paganism."[2] Classical studies, meaning the study of the pagan authors, became the rage. One could tell the difference between an educated man and one who was not by the fact that the educated man knew classical Greek and Latin and was acquainted with the pagan writers and pagan mythology. Ovid, Seneca, and Cicero replaced Augustine and Chrysostom in the curriculum. Schoolboys still studied the Bible, but they also studied Homer. Greek history was as important as English history. Writers assumed their readers had an easy familiarity with Pericles and the Golden Age, the tale of the Spartan boy who hid the fox in his cloak, the Peloponnesian Wars, and Julius Caesar's campaigns in Gaul. Greek and Roman styles were revived in drama, sculpture, painting, language, and especially architecture.

All this would have only historical interest were it not for several other major changes that occurred around the same time. One was the Protestant Reformation. Harold Lindsell, former editor of *Christianity Today* and himself a Protestant (as we are), plainly states his opinion that:

[The Reformation] was a major factor in opening the door wide to the Enlightenment of the eighteenth century. . . .

Once the Protestant churches claimed their freedom to dis-sent and freedom to believe other than what was taught by Rome, they opened the doors to wider dissent and to irre-ligion as well. . . . The very notion of religious freedom of necessity included the right to disseminate and to propa-gate religious ideas of every sort, whether they were in accord with community standards or not. This dangerous precedent had its roots in the Reformation and was to bring forth its own fruit in the years ahead. Since religious freedom has implications in the fields of economics, poli-tics, and social life and behavior, there was no church that could render compelling decisions to determine what the civilization of a people should or would be.[3]

In other words, the Reformation led eventually to a the-ory of *religious toleration*. Since the competing religions were all brands of Christianity, no real need was seen for setting bounds on which religions could be tolerated. That led, in turn, to a philosophy of *complete* religious toleration. But complete religious toleration, taken to its logical conclusion, means that *paganism cannot be outlawed*. As we will see, this would lead to unexpected results in future centuries.

Another result of the Reformation was that *the church let go of education*. As Lindsell also mentions, "Education [before the Reformation] had been a church function. . . . There was no education to speak of that was not involved with reli-gion."[4] Concerned with fighting tyranny in the church, the Reformers sometimes went overboard in handing power to the State. With the church no longer the guardian of educa-tion, pagans had a brand-new opportunity to promote their ideas to the young.

It was not long before "free-thinking," formerly the exclusive province of the secret societies, became a move-ment in its own right. Claiming to be motivated solely by logic, philosophers such as Voltaire and Rousseau in France and Locke and Hume in England began to develop theories of man, righteousness, and government that deliberately were *not* based on the Bible. They accused their opponents of unintelligent fanaticism and a mere willingness to believe not based on reason. This movement, called by its followers "The Enlightenment," but which more aptly should be called "The Endarkenment," is at the root of the pagan revival today.

> By the middle of the eighteenth century, there was a clearly defined and significant movement in process that has been called the Enlightenment. . . . This movement in two centuries was to do what it took the church at Pentecost three centuries to do. It would reverse what the early church had done and bring to Europe and to the West in general the New Paganism; this New Paganism has dislodged the church from its key religious and cultural position.[5]

> While the victory of the Enlightenment did not erase the church from history and the West, it did unseat the church from its primary position in Western civilization and break its hold by installing a new Westanschauung [worldview] that stood in opposition to Christianity, and that in turn brought the West under the control of a new Zeitgeist [literally "time-spirit"; we would call this "moral climate" or even "lifestyle"] that was secular and anti-Christian.[6]

Some would say, "How can this be? How could a movement devoted to reason have anything to do with promoting paganism?" Good question, and here's the good answer.

In order to reason and use logic, you have to start somewhere. One writer, such as Rousseau, might start from the proposition, "Nature is good and we should learn from her." Another might start with the idea, "Survival is the highest duty of the human race." Still another might begin by arguing, as B. F. Skinner does, that a smoothly working society is the highest good. *None of these people can prove that his starting point is correct by using logic.* We well could argue that nature is cruel, and men are not animals so we need not imitate the animals; that survival is *not* the highest duty of the human race; and that if we all are machines (as B. F. Skinner also asserts), who cares if society runs smoothly or not?

The Enlightenment philosophers had a naive belief in the power of human reason to produce logical starting points. They grievously underestimated the contribution that a shared Christian heritage made to their own thinking. The whole question of right and wrong, for instance, is not found in Hindu thinking, yet these philosophers spent hours arguing which form of society was right and which was wrong. They also underestimated the effect of their own wishes and desires on their "logical" philosophical systems. A man who wants to commit adultery, for example, has a vested interest in "proving" the illogic of monogamous marriage.

Men need Scripture to provide the absolute principles that men *cannot* reason out by pure logic. Enlightenment thinkers also underestimated the spiritual side of man: his conscience, sense of eternity, and need for God. However, they did manage to trap the church into a futile effort to prove the truth of the Bible *from logic alone*, although the Bible itself recommends relying on the power of the Holy Spirit and the conviction of the individual conscience, along with the testimony of the written Word.

What the church did, and has kept on doing, was to concede the point that truth could not be proved *absolutely*. The Enlightenment corollary was that nobody should be taught truth at all. Each person should be left free to "decide for himself" what to believe. Anything else was sheer fanatical indoctrination. However, indoctrinating young children in Enlightenment beliefs was simply "teaching them to think and reason on their own."

People have natural spiritual needs, and the Enlightenment could not obliterate these. What it did accomplish was to make a belief in absolute truth unfashionable. This, of course, was no bar at all to believing in or amusing oneself with the pagan gods, whose religion never claimed to be the One True Way. As Harold Lindsell noted, "The Enlightenment steeped itself in the writings of the Greco-Roman world into which Christianity entered at Pentecost."[7] This was the spirit of classical paganism: tolerant of all beliefs except the belief that there was only one right belief, proud of its ability to reason and act, totally hostile to all moral restraints.

In a very real sense, the mission of the Enlightenment was to turn the clock back to early Rome — a Rome without Christians.

First Fruits of the Enlightenment

The fruit of the Enlightenment was immediate and bitter. Prominent Enlightenment writers got together and produced the French *Encyclopédie*, the first attempt to build a monument in words to the achievements of men. Almost needless to say, the *Encyclopédie* was rabidly anti-Christian. As Lindsell says, "Its content . . . ran counter to everything intrinsic to a culture and civilization based on the Hebrew-Christian tradition." Based on the *Encyclopédie* and other Enlightenment writings, the French launched their disastrous Revolution. Meanwhile, across the Channel, without the benefit of any revolution, the common Englishman got more rights and justice than the common French worker, thanks to the Methodist revival, which we have already mentioned.

But the French Revolution was just the beginning.

Once the elite had closed their minds to Biblical revelation, they almost immediately began falling for every spiritual con game and fringe teaching around.

In the United States, it took until the 1840s for Enlightenment thinking to make any serious inroads. The people had been so heavily Christianized that even the secret society members were more Christian in their outlook than many Christians today. George Washington, for example, although a Mason, had a strongly Christian view of the role of government.

Fakers and Frauds

The first big coup for paganism in the USA was the séance fad, started by the Fox family of Hydesville, New York. The Fox girls, who years later confessed to having faked the whole thing, conducted table-rapping sessions during which ghosts supposedly answered the questions of the people around the table. In spite of the almost continuous exposés of fake mediums, "it persisted as a mass phenomenon into the 1920s,"[8] and longer across the sea in Great Britain and other countries. The upper class was particularly susceptible to its appeal; British writers like mystery doyen Dame Agatha Christie featured séances and contact with the ghosts of the dead in their books, and even the humor writer P. G. Wodehouse found it such a prominent feature of upper-class society that many of his stories feature batty spiritualistic ladies.

Séances were just the kickoff, though. In the mid-1800s, literally dozens of new cults would explode onto the American scene. Often founded by women (see 1 Timothy 2:14 and 2 Timothy 3:6), these cults claimed great new spiritual revelations. Teaching the same doctrines as the pagan secret societies, these new cults counted on the American doctrine of complete religious toleration to enable them to come out in the open. In a few cases, notably that of Mormonism, the cult's doctrine was so violently opposed to Christian practice that parts of it were outlawed. The Mormons, for example, had to jettison polygamy before Utah could join the Union.

The cults, however, all claimed to fall in the Christian tradition. The founders were *interpreting* the Bible or *retranslating* the Bible or *discovering hidden books* of the Bible. Not yet had paganism *as paganism* been seriously promoted in the USA.

The First American New Age

The Theosophical Society changed all that. Headed by the somber, heavy-eyebrowed Madame Blavatsky, the T.S. of the mid-1800s featured major exploits of channeling. Madame Blavatsky supposedly was in touch with "an Egyptian group of the Universal Mystic Brotherhood" and "Tibetan Masters," all through the miracle of time-warp telepathy. After seven embarrassing years in India, during which the British Psychical Society unmasked many favorite T.S. practices as total frauds, Blavatsky headed for England, where she spent her time promoting her books and her organization.

Meanwhile, back in the USA, a series of scandals resulted in the coming to power of Annie Besant, a lady of similar personality and beliefs to Margaret Sanger, the founder of Planned Parenthood. With an avant-garde elitist type in control, T. S. gained social respectability among the upper class, a respectability not at all diminished by the sex scandals that so freely circulated about its leaders. It was fashionable to twiddle with channeling and natter about the Ancient Wisdom of the Ages (meaning the Society's sanitized version of Hinduism). After all, Who Knows What Awaits Us on the Other Side of the Veil? We Must be Open to the Leading of the Spirits . . . etc., etc. Good stuff for cocktail parties, and it fit right in with the increasing degeneracy of the upper class.

Many of us today do not realize how debauched upperclass Americans of the 1920s were. This was the era when Margaret Sanger was promoting free sex, when the first miniskirts came in, when girls cast off the role of future housewife and paraded as flappers, when couples danced all night and got drunk at speakeasy saloons. Men, in a frenzy of greed, were amassing huge debts in order to make a killing on the stock market. Young couples, for the first time in the history of the world, were setting off on unchaperoned dates, thanks to the new crop of permissive parents and Henry Ford's mass production of the Model T. The market for birth control was wide open. This was the time when the Theosophical Society successfully introduced reincarnation, karma, "planes of consciousness," bodily auras, chakras, and other pagan concepts — "all concepts that have been embraced by New Age groups." As Jay Kinney points out in his marvelous article "Déja Vu: The Hidden History of the New Age," "In many cases, books published by Theosophical publishers on these subjects were the first of their kind."[9]

The upper class was jaded. It was looking for new kicks. It got them, but not in the way it had expected. God had mercy on America. He sent the Depression.

The Depression Knocks Back the New Age

The first effect of the stock market crash was a rapid decline in the market for occult and immoral teachings. Faced with the need to come back from disaster, America was not in a mood to play funny mind games. Life had become serious again. People simply couldn't *afford* to act like libertines.

Various minor occult leaders carried on the work of promoting paganism, but it was heavy sledding. Guy Ballard, the leader of the "I Am" movement of the Thirties, died unexpectedly — a heavy blow, since he said he *wasn't* going to die, but "ascend." His widow got zapped for mail fraud the next year "and the mighty 'I Am' movement soon became 'I Was,' " in the well-chosen words of Jay Kinney![10] Alice Bailey and her husband, Foster, kept busy churning out New Age books, but she died in 1949, too early to collect big royalties from today's large sales of these tedious tomes. A few other scattered weirdos did their best, but found it hard to make a living at it anywhere but California.

Prosperity Returns, and Here Comes the New Age Again

Not until prosperity returned in the 1950s did the New Age once again hold out reasonable possibilities for a lucrative career. Mark and Elizabeth Clare Prophet picked up where the "I Am"-ers had left off and managed to make a decent living at it. Spiritualists in England managed to get the laws against witchcraft and occult activity repealed, and various witches crawled out of the woodwork to go on speaking tours. Still paganism was a small-scale activity that did not look good on a business resumé, until the youth rebellion of the 1960s finally produced a large crop of monied youngsters ready to adopt any teaching that flattered them and insulted their parents. Many of them moved to California, giving them even greater exposure to the "heavy teachings" of the assorted gurus, swamis, channelers, healers, and so on recommended by their favorite rock stars. This group of sixties kids is now the backbone of the New Age movement, such as it is.

We say, "such as it is," because the actual core of true believers appears to be much smaller than the number of people willing to amuse themselves with New Age teachings. Jim and Selena Fox, who run "the largest pagan network in the United States," and who publish the quarterly newspaper *Circle Network News*, need to print only three thousand copies. This newspaper "reaches a substantial section of the American pagan community, estimated variously at between 40,000 and 50,000 practicing adherents."[11] Of course, these are hard-core pagans, not your average New Age tripper, and the New Age influence can't be measured solely in terms of dedicated believers. As long as outsiders allow themselves to be leavened by New Age teaching, they will find themselves drifting further and further toward classical paganism.

The Pagans are Accrediting the Christians

Again, this would not necessarily be a matter for full-scale alarm *if* education in America were in the hands of the people. But it is not. For the most part, education is controlled by the state. Specifically, the teacher's colleges indoctrinate every public school teacher in the country in the latest "educational theories" (meaning the latest fashionable beliefs about the nature of man). The National Education Association (NEA), which by now is thoroughly committed to anti-Christian principles, controls most state legislatures. State universities are now controlled by feminists, New Agers, and Marxists. In practice, this means that, under the guise of "religious neutrality," public school and university students are indoctrinated in the pet beliefs of the elite.[12]

At first this meant American children were trained in Enlightenment thinking, i.e., secular humanism. Today it means children are participating in nature-worship rites under the guise of "studying Native American culture"; reading the *Book of Shadows,* a publication of the Church of Wicca (witchcraft); learning to call up demons through the process of "stress management" (actually, Eastern meditation) and "finding the wise person inside yourself"; and more abuses than we have room to mention.

Parents complain, but usually in vain. The education elite is convinced that it will save the planet by indoctrinating children in New Age ideals. If this is allowed to continue for a few more years, the small number of New Agers will be swelled by literally millions and millions of young adults who have been taught to *unquestioningly* believe in New Age teachings, and by thousands and thousands of "good Christian teachers" who have unsuspectingly imbibed New Age teaching in the teacher's colleges.

Believe it or not, all this is our inheritance from the Enlightenment.

From the Enlightenment we got the idea of giving leadership to the "learned man," meaning the person with a degree from an Enlightenment-approved institution. It was the beginning of the Age of the Expert, and strangely enough the only place an American could get a doctorate was at an overseas university — more often than not, the Enlightenment-controlled universities of Germany.[13] Armed with these formidable credentials, the fledgling convert to Enlightenment thinking could then count on a career spent amazing the natives with his deep erudition, which certainly sounded like nothing they had ever heard from Preacher Jones.

Gradually the idea spread through all American society that you had to have an accredited degree to do almost anything. This meant that if you could just get degrees for *your* guys and put them in charge of the universities, you had the biggest captive audience in the country for your teaching. John Dewey, the famous educator and originator of the *Humanist Manifesto,* followed exactly that strategy — and his followers took over the entire American education system.

The American public education system (including state universities) is now the biggest unacknowledged church in the country — and the majority of Christians send their children to it. *And* Christians are forbidden by Supreme Court ruling from using the public schools to teach Christian doctrine, whereas New Agers are not. *They* know how to make their occult teachings sound "scientific" and "neutral." Channeling sessions can be recast as "helping the students get in touch with their inner selves." Pagan worship rituals are recast as a means to "overcome prejudice against other races," or even as a way to teach children about that great American virtue, religious diversity. On the other hand, there is no way that the doctrine of Christ coming to sacrifice Himself on behalf of sinners can be smuggled in as a psychological self-help device.

The ACLU is now even protesting the teaching of Christian morality — e.g., that marriage is better than fornication. While the school door is wide open to the New Age, it slammed shut in Christians' faces decades ago.

Enlightenment types also preached *modernism* — the doctrine that nothing your father or his father believed amounts to a hill of beans — while conveniently ignoring the fact that *their* own beliefs came from ancient Greece and Rome. Under the banner of Progress, they were able to accomplish amazing feats, such as dismantling the entire system of church and private schools in America and replacing them with public schools run according to Enlightenment principles. Since then, by preaching *religious toleration* they have managed to eliminate the religion of Christianity from the government schools, and almost from all public life as well. So today it is literally easier to teach a class on witchcraft and have the children conduct a séance than to teach a class on Christianity and have the children say a prayer to the God of the Bible. If you do the first, the ACLU won't say a word. If you do the latter, all Hell will most literally break loose.

Christians thus find themselves in the strange dilemma of believing in religious freedom and yet seeing that this makes it very difficult to suppress ugly religions and practices.

What is the answer? Are we just doomed to see the New Age elite take over the reins of power while we are prevented from lifting a finger by "the separation of church and state"?

Let's see.

AN END TO EVIL EMPIRES, OR EVERYTHING YOU REALLY NEED TO KNOW ABOUT THE NEW AGE YOU LEARNED IN SUNDAY SCHOOL

God, have you cast us away?
Have you spurned us?
You go not forth with our armies;
your help, O God, grant us.
Fighting the enemy man's help is empty.
But with God we strive with valor.
He tramples down our foes!

—Psalm 108:10–13,
from the *Book of Psalms for Singing*

We have good new and bad news. First, the bad news. Times have changed.

The Western nations used to have a Christian culture. Most people belonged, with varying degrees of sincerity, to some established Christian church in which the gospel was preached a whole lot more pointedly than it is nowadays. Everyone knew the Ten Commandments; they were posted on classroom walls. Government buildings had Scriptures inscribed into their stone arches. The laws were also unselfconsciously Christian. You knew the government was committed to fighting murder and rape, for instance. That helped, because any religion that did such things could be outlawed on account of its practices without ever referring to its religious aspects.

Today, with the leaders of society proudly proclaiming their commitment to abortion rights, infanticide, euthanasia, sexual immorality, pornography, and the like, it is no longer possible to count on this Christian moral consensus. If a group of people appeared in court claiming their right to sacrifice living aborted fetuses as an offering to their goddess, it is not possible to predict which way the court would rule.

Why Should We Let Them Make the Rules?

That was the bad news. Now here's the good news. *Christians do not have to play the game according to the pagans' rules.* The rule that *all* religions, even Satan worship, must be

193

given equal treatment under the law is not in the Bible. The rule that we must not hurt the fragile self-esteem of non-believers by pointing out their evil practices and ungodly beliefs is not in the Bible. The rule that we must obey Supreme Court decisions that forbid our children to pray in school is not in the Bible. The rule that we must not impose our morality on other people is definitely not in the Bible!

The whole point of civil government is to impose morality on unwilling people. If nobody disliked the government's rules, there would be no need for government. The question just is, *Whose* morality? Pagans have morals, too, even if they don't like to use the word, and they do their best to impose them on everyone else. The same people who are so worried about Christians imposing our morality on them support compulsory attendance laws, compulsory organ donation laws, compulsory sex education, and censorship of Christian practice in the public arena.

What pagans really mean by, "Don't impose your morality on us," is "Let there be no limits to our tyranny." If there is no absolute Law of God saying, "Thou shalt not murder," then rulers and their henchmen can murder all they like. If no law says, "Thou shalt not commit adultery," then the elite can corrupt our sons and daughters at will. If "Thou shalt not steal" is no longer an unbreakable rule, then you can bet the elite will take bribes, confiscate property, and use their power in every way they can to enrich themselves. This is *exactly* what has happened in *every* country where the rulers have cast away God's Law. And what happens then to those who protest this oppression? They end up at the guillotine or in the gulag.

Please remember this — there is no more important point in this book: *True freedom is only possible for the people when both they and the rulers are bound by the same righteous, unchanging, absolute laws.* Only when you can be sure that the ruler is held accountable to *not* steal, *not* commit adultery, *not* lie, and so on, can you have any confidence that he will not be imposing his lusts on you. As long as the ruler gets to make up whatever rules he wants, he cannot be held accountable by anyone. In Biblical terms, he has declared himself a god, just as Caesar was declared a god in ancient Rome.

America's Founding Fathers were keenly alive to the possibility of despots arising who would want to play god. That is why they made such an effort to promote total freedom for Christianity in their new republic. As George Washington said in his famous Farewell Address, religion and morality are the two "great pillars of human happiness . . . nor can it be expected that national morality can prevail in exclusion of religous principle." By which he surely meant that there *were* absolute religious principles, namely those of traditional nondenominational Christianity, which the country should follow.

"Oh," some will protest, "surely the 'freedom of religion' mentioned in the Bill of Rights means the founders intended to create a free bazaar of religions, where everything from Satanism to Ba'hai gets equal protection." Not a chance.

We would like to suggest that what the Founding Fathers meant by "freedom of religion" was "freedom of Biblical religion," e.g., Christianity and its associated sects. They were worried that one of these sects might become an established state religion, but not at all opposed to generally promoting Christianity. As Supreme Court Justice Joseph Story, who served from 1811 to 1845, wrote,

Probably at the time of the adoption of the Constitution, and of the first amendment to it . . . the general if not the universal sentiment in America was, that Christianity ought to receive encouragement from the state so far as was not incompatible with the private rights of conscience and the freedom of religious worship. An attempt to level all religions, and to make it a matter of state policy to hold all in utter indifference, would have created universal disapprobation, if not universal indignation. . . . The real object of the amendment was not to countenance, much less to advance, Mahometanism, or Judaism, or infidelity, by prostrating Christianity; but to exclude all rivalry among Christian sects, and to prevent any national ecclesiastical establishment which should give to a hierarchy the exclusive patronage of the national government.[1]

America was intended to be a Christian nation with its laws based on the Bible. This would avoid the anarchy of having *no* settled authority on which to base the laws. For, in fact, if you study early American law it is crystal-clear that it *was* based on the Bible. Others have written at length in proof of these points, and if you wish to study the proofs further we list a number of sources in the footnotes.[2]

We don't have long to say this, and we're only going to say it once: *The idea of total religious freedom is a myth.* There is no such thing as a country without a state religion (which is *not* the same thing as a state denomination!). The louder a country proclaims its commitment to religious neutrality, the surer you can be that you will find a system of rigorous indoctrination in the *undeclared* religion.

America and the other Western nations are inevitably going to be either Christian or pagan. We have to choose which. If we don't choose, the choice will be made for us.

What Will Happen
If We Keep Playing by Their Rules

In all of history, all pagan empires have had the choice of only two fates:
(1) Surrender to the Lord.
(2) Be used by God to judge His unfaithful people . . . and then be crushed.
If the church refuses to fight paganism on God's terms, we can accurately predict what will happen. The Western church will be severely judged, and then the Western nations will be destroyed, while the Lord raises up more faithful followers for Himself in Russia, China, Nigeria, or some other

presently unlikely place. If the church does stand and fight, we can also tell you what will happen. There will be a period of persecution. Some of us will be thrown in jail. Others might even be killed. Yet others will be threatened with the loss of their property. But if we stand firm, either the Lord will take us all away (through death or otherwise!) and then judge the culture which refuses to hear us, or He will give us back our country.

You can see this process going on right now with Operation Rescue, the pro-life rescue movement that closes down abortion clinics by massive sit-ins. (This is not civil disobedience, by the way, since an unconstitutional law is illegal, and the laws legalizing abortion and preventing pro-lifers from giving information to abortion-bound women are egregiously unconstitutional, no matter what the Supreme Court says.) These rescuers have been jailed, beaten, and threatened with massive lawsuits. But they are following the Scriptural path of standing firm "as one man" contending for the truth. According to the Bible, this is a sign to nonbelievers that Operation Rescue will be delivered, but that God will destroy its opposition, as long as the rescuers remain faithful and courageous (Philippians 1:27–29).

Seven Strategies for Overcoming the New Age

The ingredients of Christian victory have never changed. Boldness. Conviction of truth and intolerance of error. Selflessness and service of others. Humility. Holiness. Hope for the future and a belief in the God who can do great things. To this we would like to add a few notes on strategy, directions Christians must take if we want to spread the gospel in our nations and not just wait to be fodder for pagan fires.

(1) Education.
Once again, education must become a church function. We mean *all* education, from kindergarten through graduate

school. We Christians cannot hope to even hold our position, let alone advance, while we hand our own children over to people imbued with pagan ideals. This means in practice that all our children should be either home-schooled or in private Christian schools run under church authority, or that somehow they must be able to get a Christian education and act like Christians in public school. Christian kids in public school should refuse to attend classes in which they are taught pagan doctrines (e.g., evolution, witchcraft, that all religions are alike) and should pray and preach exactly as if the Supreme Court had never met the ACLU. The wonderful Christian public school teachers we hear so much about should also liberate their lights from under the bushel and feel free to explain the Christian point of view on any subject, pray with and for the children, run Bible studies, and so on.

(2) Media and entertainment.

It is time for Christians to stop supporting media that insult Christians and Christ and promote paganism. How can we win, or even hang in there, while we let *them* preach to us six hours a day and *we* are not available to preach to them because we are too busy listening to *their* message? This applies to, but is not limited to, both network and public TV, magazine subscriptions, newspapers, movies, radio shows, music, and live entertainment. It is now possible to purchase a video player that does not tune in TV, and we strongly suggest Christian families junk their TV sets and get one of these. As for news, we have plenty of good Christian media that will be happy to supply even more of it if we would just support them.

(3) Apologetics.

It's time to stop trying to prove the truth of Christianity on pagan terms and start treating them to a taste of the power of God. Christians should stop presenting medical ethics in terms of "It really is cheaper to save handicapped people than to kill them" and legal ethics in terms of the cost of prison construction. We know what is *right*. Let's admit it is *right.* Let's talk about selflessness and justice and what the Bible says about current issues. Let's also stop flinching away from the prospect of being called unloving and judgmental. New Agers define love as totally accepting people as they are and never pressuring them to change their evil ways. So they are going to call us unloving. Let's not go along with this and actually *be* unloving by letting them travel unimpeded down the road to Hell.

(4) Evangelism.
Let our preachers start believing that five thousand really can be converted by a single sermon in a single hour. Let's stop fiddle-faddling with church growth statistics and demographics and projecting our niddling little 2 percent per annum church growth rate out into the future. When a denominational spokesman makes an outrageously faithless statement like calling "pure fantasy" the idea that your denomination will eventually surpass the size of the liberal Presbyterian Church, saying "continued growth is not expected and is not realistic," call him on the carpet.[3]

(5) Family productivity.
Let's stop treating the Christian family as some pathological growth and start *training* it. If we could simply manage to have more than the average 1.8 children *and raise them to be Christians,* we would eventually overtake the pagan element with our numbers, *even without evangelism.* The church should make it top priority to train parents to train their children how to train *their* children.

(6) Church leadership.
The church should also rigorously enforce the Biblical standards for church leaders, and make it a goal to train every man not disqualified because of divorce to become an elder, and his wife to be an elder's wife. If this were done consistently for one generation, it would go far to eliminate the divorce plague in our churches.

(7) Government.

Throwing all our efforts into electing "our" guys is *not* the best way to advance our cause. Taking away the market for government intervention by doing the job ourselves *is*. So is standing up for what is right even if it does cut into our Social Security checks. We will find support in government for our goals if we are willing to put our money where our mouths are.

Strategies for how to accomplish most of these goals are discussed in Mary Pride's book *All the Way Home* (Crossway Books, 1989) and Bill Pride's *Flirting with the Devil* (Crossway Books, 1988). All we're asking from you right now is a commitment to these goals, and a belief that God can help us meet them.

We Shall Overcome!

A motley collection of fishermen, tax collectors, and illiterate Galileans took over the Roman Empire. A group of insignificant young men kicked off a revival that changed the face of England and America. God wiped out the Assyrian armies surrounding Jerusalem. All of this can happen again today. All we have to do is take what we learned in Sunday school about missionaries converting pagan tribes and *apply it to our own country*. Challenge the idols. Teach them the Ten Commandments. Tell them the gospel. Do what you can to replace ungood pagan laws and social structures with good, sound, time-tested Christian laws and social structures. And *whatever* you do, don't go around repeating the lie that pagan beliefs and practices are just as valid as Christian beliefs and practices! Don't make a bargain to leave them alone if they'll leave you alone. (For one thing, they won't keep it.) We are not here to hold people's hands until they arrive safely in Hell, but to show them the way to Heaven.

This is why you got saved: not to hold down a pew until the New Agers come and take it away, but to serve in the

Lord's army. God has given us our weapons: not physical swords and tanks, but prayer, holy living, and bold preaching of righteousness.

New Agers may have their thousands of books, but we have our one Book that is worth more than all of them put together. They may have the media, educators, and even many lawmakers in their pockets, but our God has the whole world in His hands. They may have their conspiracies, but no conspiracy can succeed against the Lord.

The New Age is here for a purpose. *God's* purpose. Those of us who have had our heads in the sand now have a chance to taste what continuing apathy will bring upon us. The New Age may be the very tool God uses to finally unite Christians of this day into an army to fight God's battles. If our fear of a pagan future is enough to pry us away from our TV sets and to get us serious about raising our kids as Christians, we will have reason to look back and bless God for letting it out into the open. But if we refuse to come when the Lord summons us and to fight as He directs, we can look forward to sharing the judgment God will rain down on our pagan culture.

The New Age is the direct result of Christian indifference. Our grandparents did this to us — now it's our duty to clean up the mess for our grandchildren.

We have done our best to give you a broom.

Now let's start sweeping!

BIBLIOGRAPHY

Books

Angus, S. *The Mystery-Religions.* New York: Dover Publications, 1975.

Bach, Marcus. *Strange Sects and Curious Cults.* Westport, CT: Greenwood Press, 1961.

Bobgan, Martin and Diedre. *PsychoHeresy.* Santa Barbara, CA: East Gate Publishers, 1987.

Brill, E. J. *The Conflict Between El and Ba'al in Canaanite Religion.* Netherlands: Leiden, 1969.

Brow, Robert. *Religion: Origins and Ideas.* 2d ed. London: Tyndale Press, 1972.

Bucke, Richard M. *Cosmic Consciousness.* New York: E. P. Dutton, 1901.

Bunce, William K. *Religions in Japan: Buddhism, Shinto, Christianity, from the report prepared by the Religions and Cultural Resources Division, Civil Information and Education Section, General Headquarters of the Supreme Commander for the Allied Powers.* Tokyo, March 1948. Rutland, VT: Charles E. Tuttle Company, 1955.

Burkert, Walter. *Greek Religion.* Cambridge, MA: Harvard University Press, 1985.

Cavendish, Richard, ed. *Encyclopedia of the Unexplained.* New York: McGraw-Hill, 1974.

Dallimore, Arnold. *George Whitefield: The Life and Times of the Great Evangelist of the Eighteenth-Century Revival.* Westchester, IL: Crossway Books, 1970.

Davies, Nigel. *Human Sacrifice in History and Today*. New York: William Morrow, 1981.

Drury, Nevill. *The Occult Experience: Magic in the New Age*. Garden City Park, NY: Avery Publishing Group, Inc., 1989.

Dumezil, Georges. *Archaic Roman Religions*. Chicago, IL: University of Chicago Press,1970.

Eliade, Mircea. *From the Stone Age to the Eleusinian Mysteries*, Vol. 1 of *A History of Religious Ideas*. Chicago: University of Chicago Press, 1978.

Matthew Fox. *Whee, Wee, We, All the Way Home . . . A Guide to a Sensual, Prophetic Spirituality*. Santa Fe, NM: Bear & Company, 1981.

Fox, Robin Lane. *Pagans and Christians*. New York: Alfred A. Knopf, Inc., 1987.

Fradenburgh, J. N. *Fire from Strange Altars*. Cincinnati, OH: Cranston & Stowe, 1891.

Gray, John. *The Canaanites*. New York: Frederick A. Praeger Publishers, 1964. Vol. 38 in the series *Ancient People and Places*.

Griscom, Chris. *Ecstacy Is a New Frequency*. Santa Fe, NM: Bear & Company, 1987.

Groothuis, Douglas. *Unmasking the New Age*. Downer's Grove, IL: InterVarsity Press, 1986.

Heider, George C. *The Cult of Molech — A Reassessment*. Sheffield, England: Journal of Old Testament Studies Press, 1985.

Hope, Murray. *Practical Celtic Magic*. New York: St. Martin's Press, 1987.

_____. *Practical Egyptian Magic*. New York: St. Martin's Press, 1984.

Howes, Michael. *Amulets*. New York: St. Martin's Press, 1975.

Jastrow, Morris, Jr. *Aspects of Religious Practice in Babylonia and Assyria*. New York: Benjamin Blom, Inc., 1911.

Kaplan, J. D., ed. *The Dialogues of Plato*. New York: Washington Square Press, 1951.

Kilpatrick, William Kirk. *Psychological Seduction*. Nashville: Thomas Nelson Publishers, 1983.

Larson, Bob. *Straight Answers on the New Age*. Nashville: Thomas Nelson Publishers, 1989.

Leon-Portilla, Miguel. *Aztec Thought and Culture*. Tulsa, OK: University of Oklahoma Press, 1963.

Lindsell, Harold. *The New Paganism: Understanding American Culture and the Role of the Church*. New York: Harper & Row, 1987.

Marrs, Texe. *Dark Secrets of the New Age*. Westchester, IL: Crossway Books, 1987.

_____. *Mystery Mark of the New Age*. Westchester, IL: Crossway Books, 1988.

Martin, Luther H. *Hellenistic Religions*. New York: Oxford University Press, 1987.

Miller, David L. *The New Polytheism: Rebirth of the Gods and Goddesses*. New York: Harper & Row, 1974.

Morley, Sylvanus GriswORD. *The Ancient Maya*. 3d ed., revised by George W. Brainerd. Stanford: Stanford University Press, 1956.

Neill, Stephen. *A History of Christian Missions*. Middlesex, England: Penguin Books, 1964.

Organ, Troy Wilson. *Hinduism*. Woodbury, NY: Barron's Educational Series, 1974.

Parrinder, Geoffrey, ed. *World Religions from Ancient History to the Present*. New York: Facts on File, 1985.

Payne, J. Barton. *An Outline of Hebrew History*. Self-published, 1954.

Price, John Randolph. *The Planetary Commission*. Austin, TX: Quartus Books, 1984.

Renou, Louis, ed. *Hinduism*. New York: George Brazillier, 1962.

Schultz, Ted, ed. *The Fringes of Reason: A Field Guide to New Age Frontiers, Unusual Beliefs and Eccentric Sciences*. New York: Harmony Books, 1989.

Seignobos, Charles. *The World of Babylon*. Translated by David Macrae. New York: Leon Amiel, Publisher, 1975.

Seligman, Kurt. *The History of Magic and the Occult*. New York: Harmony Books, 1975.

Silverberg, Robert. *The Man Who Found Nineveh.* New York: Holt, Rinehart and Winston, 1964.

Skinner, B. F. *Beyond Freedom and Dignity.* New York: Bantam Books, 1971.

Smith, John Holland. *The Death of Classical Paganism.* New York: Charles Scribner's Sons, 1976.

Timms, Moira. *Prophecies and Predictions: Everyone's Guide to the Coming Changes.* Santa Cruz, CA: Unity Press, 1980.

Volz, Carl A. *The Church of the Middle Ages: Growth and Change from 600 to 1400.* St. Louis: Concordia Publishing House, 1970.

Walker, Barbara G. *The Skeptical Feminist — Discovering the Virgin, Mother, and Crone.* San Francisco: Harper & Row, 1987.

White, Jon Manchip. *Cortez and the Downfall of the Aztec Empire.* New York: St. Martin's Press, 1971.

Wilkins, J. Steven. *America: The First 350 Years.* Forest, MS: Covenant Publications, 1988.

Wood, Garth. *The Myth of Neurosis.* New York: Harper & Row, 1986.

Yogi, Maharishi Mahesh. *Inauguration of the Dawn of the Age of Enlightenment.* Fairfield, IA: Maharishi International University Press, 1975.

Encyclopedias

The 1987 World Book Year Book. Chicago: World Book, Inc., 1987.

The New Encyclopedia Britannica. 15th ed. Chicago: Encyclopedia, Inc., 1988.

Magazines, Newspapers, and Journals

The Journal of Humanistic Psychology.
The Light of Olympia, Vol. 1, No. 10, October 1988.
The New Age Catalogue.
The New Times. August 1988, February 1989.

The Practical Mystic. Winter 1988.
Psychic Guide Magazine. September-November 1986.
Spiritual Women's Times. Spring 1988.
The Transformation Times. January 1989.

NOTES

INTRODUCTION

1. Subtitled, "A complete manual of Egyptian magical practices, including safe and simple rituals adapted for present-day use." Murray Hope (New York: St. Martin's Press, 1984).
2. Subtitled, "A working guide to the magical traditions of the Celts." Murray Hope (Wellingborough, Northamptonshire, England: The Aquarian Press, 1987).
3. Of course these pathways are no longer secret, thanks to author Thomas E. Mails. (Tulsa, OK: Council Oak Books, 1988).
4. José Arguelles (Santa Fe, NM: Bear & Co, 1987).
5. The people who brought us *The Whole Earth Catalog* and its younger siblings, for example, point out in their new book *Fringes of Reason*, "Although marketing categories such as 'New Age music' and 'New Age books' may be recent arrivals on the scene, the New Age itself is hardly new. Nearly every spiritual or cultural phenomenon associated with the term dates back at least several generations. . . ." *The Fringes of Reason* (New York: Harmony Books, 1989), p. 22. They also complain of a sense of "*déja vu*" and monotony when comparing today's "New" Age to the "new" spiritualism of a hundred years ago (p. 167).
6. *Fringes of Reason*, p. 65.
7. *Fringes of Reason*, p. 32, debunks these claims.

CHAPTER ONE: A Quickie Field Guide to the New Age

1. Susan Wooldridge, "Inner Guide Meditation for East and West," *The Practical Mystic*, Winter 1988, p. 22.
2. *The New Encylopædia Britannica*, Vol. 25, p. 89.
3. Krysta Gibson, "An Interview with Elliot James," *The New Times*, August 1988, p. 1.
4. "The Soul's Journey: Excerpts from a Dialogue with Kay Ries," *The New Times*, February 1989, p. 5.
5. "Body-Mind Integration in Prose, "*The New Times*, February 1989, p. 16.
6. James E. Faubel, "The Laws of Magick," *Transformation Times*, January 1989, p. 34.

7. Eileen Shavelson, "An Interview with Vicki Noble," *Spiritual Women's Times,* Spring 1988, p. 2.
8. Maharishi Mahesh Yogi, for example, teaches that he established a New Age of Enlightenment in 1975 and that those who do not belong to it are unenlightened.
9. Full-page ad by New Age activists in *Psychic Guide* magazine, September-November 1986, p. 5.
10. *Ibid.*
11. John Randolph Price, *The Planetary Commission* (Austin, TX: Quartus Books, 1984), pp. 28–32.
12. Matthew Fox, *Whee, Wee, We, all the Way Home . . . A Guide to a Sensual, Prophetic Spirituality* (Santa Fe, NM: Bear & Company, 1981), p. 242.
13. Moira Timms, *Prophecies and Predictions: Everyone's Guide to the Coming Changes* (Santa Cruz, CA: Unity Press, 1980), pp. 129–131.
14. Richard M. Bucke, *Cosmic Consciousness* (New York: E. P. Dutton, 1901).
15. Maharishi Mahesh Yogi, *Inauguration of the Dawn of the Age of Enlightenment* (Fairfield, IA: Maharishi International University Press, 1975), p. 47.
16. Price, *The Planetary Commission,* pp. 163, 164.
17. Nevill Drury,*The Occult Experience: Magic in the New Age* (Garden City Park, NY: Avery Publishing Group, Inc., 1989), p. 18.
18. James E. Faubel, "The Laws of Magick," *Transformation Times,* January 1989, p. 34.
19. Shakti Gawain, "Basics of Creative Visualization," *The New Age Catalogue,* p. 47.
20. *The Humanist Manifesto I,* Eighth Affirmation.
21. *The Humanist Manifesto I,* Twelfth Affirmation.
22. *The Humanist Manifesto I,* First, Second, and Fifth Affirmations.
23. Taken from Douglas R. Groothuis, *Unmasking the New Age* (Downers Grove, IL: InterVarsity Press, 1986), pp. 85, 86.
24. B. F. Skinner, *Beyond Freedom and Dignity* (New York: Bantam Books, 1971).
25. Three of these are:

    PsychoHeresy, Martin and Diedre Bobgan, East Gate Publishers, Santa Barbara, CA, 1987
    The Myth of Neurosis, Garth Wood, Harper & Row, New York, 1986
    Psychological Seduction, William Kirk Kilpatrick, Thomas Nelson Publishers, New York, 1983

CHAPTER TWO: *Babylon Hollywood*

1. Morris Jastrow, Jr, *Aspects of Religious Practice in Babylonia and Assyria* (New York: Benjamin Blom, 1911), p. 260.
2. J.N. Fradenburgh, *Fire from Strange Altars* (Cincinnati, OH: Cranston & Stowe, 1891), pp. 64, 65.
3. *Fire from Strange Altars,* p. 54.
4. *Fire from Strange Altars,* p. 54.

1, 132.

...lletin of Washington University in St. ...nd listings for several courses featur- ...ditions" and their "significance for ...ese courses have only become *more*

...York: St. Martin's Press, 1975), pp. 53,

Babylon. Translated by David Macrae ...er, 1975), pp. 8, 9, 11.

..., p. 68.
..., p. 67.
...The whole story is found in the fourth chapter of the Book of Daniel.

15. *Fire from Strange Altars*, pp. 46, 48, 49.
16. *Fire from Strange Altars*, p. 92.
17. Sayce, Hibbert Lectures, 1887, pp. 266, 267; as quoted in *Fire from Strange Altars*, pp. 131, 132.
18. Seignobos, *The World of Babylon*, p. 97.
19. *Fire from Strange Altars*, p. 40.
20. A. R. W. Green, *The Role of Human Sacrifice in the Ancient Near East*, p. 86.
21. Nigel Davies, *Human Sacrifice in History and Today* (New York: William Morrow, 1981), p. 13.
22. Davies, *Human Sacrifice* , pp. 289, 290.

CHAPTER THREE: *Assyria, the Armpit of the New Age*

1. Charles Seignobos, *The World of Babylon*. Translated by David Macrae (New York: Leon Amiel, Publisher, 1975), p. 23.
2. Seignobos, *The World of Babylon.*, pp. 42, 43.
3. Seignobos, *The World of Babylon.*, pp. 44, 45.
4. Silverberg, Robert, *The Man Who Found Nineveh* (New York: Holt, Rinehart and Winston, 1964), p. 145.
5. 2 Kings 18:17-19ff.
6. Seignobos, *The World of Babylon*, p. 65.
7. Seignobos, p. 112.

CHAPTER FOUR: *Way Down in Egypt Land*

1. *Aspects of Religious Practice*, pp. 15, 24.
2. *Fire from Strange Altars*, p. 295.
3. *Fire from Strange Altars*, p. 256.
4. *The New Times*, Vol. 4, No. 2, July 1988, p. 16.
5. *Strange Sects and Curious Cults*, pp. 28, 29.
6. *Strange Sects and Curious Cults*, pp. 30, 31, 33, 34.
7. *Fire from Strange Altars*, p. 288.
8. Murray Hope, *Practical Egyptian Magic* (New York: St. Martin's Press, 1984), p. 32.

CHAPTER FIVE: *In Canaan Land (It's Not So Grand)*

1. *Strange Sects and Curious Cults,* p. 12.
2. *Strange Sects and Curious Cults,* pp. 13, 14.
3. *Ibid.*
4. Barbara G. Walker, *The Skeptical Feminist — Discovering the Virgin, Mother, and Crone* (New York: Harper & Row, San Francisco, 1987), pp. 268-270.
5. *Fire from Strange Altars,* pp. 130, 131
6. *The Skeptical Feminist,* p. 270.
7. *Strange Sects and Curious Cults,* pp. 15, 16.
8. *Ibid.*
9. *The New Encyclopedia Britannica,* Vol. 24, p. 64.
10. Eliade, Mircea, *A History of Religious Ideas,* Vol. 1, *From the Stone Age to the Eleusinian Mysteries* (Chicago: University of Chicago Press, 1978), p. 155.
11. *Strange Sects and Curious Cults,* p. 17.
12. *Transformation Times,* Vol. 7, No. 9, January 1989.
13. Jeremiah 19:4-6.
14. *Fire from Strange Altars,* p. 180.
15. I Kings 18:21.
16. The whole story is found in 1 Kings 17:1, 18:1–46.
17. *The Conflict Between El and Ba'al in Canaanite Religion,* E.J. Brill, Leiden, Netherlands, 1969, Preface.

CHAPTER SIX: *Jerusalem Babylon*

1. Jeremiah 2:11
2. Exodus 34:11-17.
3. Deuteronomy 12:30, 31.
4. Joshua 17:13.
5. Judges 7.
6. Judges 11:30-40.
7. Deuteronomy 18:10, 11.
8. 1 Samuel 8:7, 8.
9. 1 Kings 11:7.
10. 2 Kings 23:10.
11. 2 Kings 21:9.
12. Luke 21:24.

CHAPTER SEVEN: *Hidden Teachings of Hinduism and Buddhism*

1. Revelation 17:5 KJV.
2. Troy Wilson Organ, *Hinduism* (Woodbury, NY: Barron's Educational Series, 1974), p. 41.
3. See chapter 10 of Texe Marrs, *Dark Secrets of the New Age* for a comprehensive, well-documented discussion of this New Age doctrine.
4. "Rationale for Good Choosing," *Journal of Humanistic Psychology,* Winter 1981.
5. Organ, *Hinduism,* p. 190.

6. Organ, *Hinduism*, p. 194.
7. Chris Griscom, *Ecstasy Is a New Frequency* (Santa Fe, NM: Bear & Company, 1987), pp. 15, 48.
8. Griscom, *Ecstasy*, p. 55.
9. *The Oregonian*, March 30, 1987, p. B-2.
10. Organ, *Hinduism*, pp. 190, 191.
11. Organ, *Hinduism*, p.192.
12. *The New Encyclopedia Britannica*, Vol. 18, p. 912.
13. Robert Brow, *Religion: Origins and Ideas* (London: Tyndale Press, second ed. 1972), pp. 27–29.
14. Brow, *Religion: Origins and Ideas*, p. 96.
15. Renou, *Hinduism*, pp. 41-43.
16. Renou, *Hinduism*, p. 31.
17. Cavendish, *Encyclopedia of the Unexplained*, pp. 242, 243.
18. Brow, *Religion: Origins and Ideas*, p. 109.
19. Davies, *Human Sacrifice*, p. 97.
20. Eliade, *A History of Religious Ideas*, Vol. 1, p. 211.
21. Eliade, *A History of Religious Ideas*, Vol. 1, pp. 211, 212.
22. Brow, *Religion: Origins and Ideas*, pp. 42, 43.
23. Brow, *Religion: Origins and Ideas*, p. 53.
24. *The New Age Catalogue*, 1988, p. 2.
25. Renou, *Hinduism*, p. 32.
26. Organ, *Hinduism*, p. 342.
27. Renou, *Hinduism*, p. 20.
28. Organ, *Hinduism*, pp. 312, 313.

CHAPTER EIGHT: *Unholy Sacrifices: Aztecs and Mayans*

1. Jon Manchip White, *Cortes and the Downfall of the Aztec Empire* (New York: St. Martin's Press, 1971), pp. 93, 94.
2. Friederich Nietzsche, *Beyond Good and Evil*, 1886, as quoted in *Cortes and the Downfall*, p. 64.
3. J. Steven Wilkins, *America: The First 350 Years* (Forest, MS: Covenant Publications, 1988), outline, p. 5.
4. White, *Cortez and the Downfall*, p. 129.
5. White, *Cortez and the Downfall*, p. 129.
6. Geoffrey Parrinder, ed., *World Religions from Ancient History to the Present* (New York: Facts on File, 1985), p. 77.
7. Parrinder, *World Religions from Ancient History to the Present*, p. 77.
8. White, *Cortez and the Downfall*, p. 114.
9. Sylvanus Griswold Morley, *The Ancient Maya* (Stanford: Stanford University Press, 1956), p. 24.
10. Morley, *The Ancient Maya*, p. 45.
11. Morley, *The Ancient Maya*, p. 163.
12. Morley, *The Ancient Maya*, p. 178.
13. Genesis 10:25.
14. Miguel Leon-Portilla, *Aztec Thought and Culture* (Tulsa, OK: University of Oklahoma Press, 1963), p. 177.
15. Parrinder, *World Religions from Ancient History to the Present*, pp. 82, 83.

16. Leon-Portilla, *Aztec Thought and Culture*, p. 73.
17. Ecclesiastes 3:21, 22 (NASB).
18. Stuart Wilde, "On the Warrior Sage," *The Light of Olympia*, Vol. 1, No. 10, October 1988, p. 13.
19. White, *Cortes and the Downfall*, pp. 83, 114.
20. White, *Cortez and the Downfall*, p. 151.
21. Thomas R. Hester, "Blood and Sacrifice: A New Look at the Maya," *The 1987 World Book Year Book* (Chicago: World Book, Inc., 1987), p. 190.
22. *Ibid.*
23. *Ibid.*
24. *Ibid.*
25. Cited in Morley, *The Ancient Maya*, p. 97.
26. Morley, *The Ancient Maya*, pp. 100, 101.
27. Morley, *The Ancient Maya*, p. 98.
28. Morley, *The Ancient Maya*, p. 99.
29. White, *Cortez and the Downfall*, p. 163.
30. White, *Cortez and the Downfall*, p. 214.

CHAPTER NINE: *Greece: The Beautiful Side of Evil*

1. J. D. Kaplan, ed., *The Dialogues of Plato* (New York: Washington Square Press, 1951), p. 316.
2. Walter Burkert, *Greek Religion* (Cambridge, MA: Harvard University Press, 1985), p. 261.
3. Luther H. Martin, *Hellenistic Religions* (New York: Oxford University Press, 1987), p. 44.
4. Martin, *Hellenistic Religions*, p. 52.
5. Martin, *Hellenistic Religions*, p. 46.
6. Martin, *Hellenistic Religions*, p. 83.
7. Martin, *Hellenistic Religions*, p. 97.
8. See, for example, David L. Miller, *The New Polytheism: Rebirth of the Gods and Goddesses* (New York: Harper & Row, 1974).
9. Albert Henry Newman, *A Manual of Church History* (Philadelphia, PA: American Baptist Publication Society, 1899, 1933), 1:20.
10. Parrinder, *World Religions from Ancient History to the Present*, p. 149.
11. Robin Lane Fox, *Pagans and Christians* (New York: Alfred A. Knopf, Inc., 1987), p. 95.
12. Parrinder, *World Religions from Ancient History to the Present*, p. 19.
13. Robert Brow, *Religion: Origins and Ideas* (London: Tyndale Press, second ed. 1972), p. 14.
14. Fox, *Pagans and Christians*, p. 110, 113.
15. Kurt Seligman, *The History of Magic and the Occult* (New York: Harmony Books, 1975), p. 48.
16. Newman, *A Manual of Church History*, 1:21.
17. Fox, *Pagans and Christians*, p. 253.
18. Harold Lindsell, *The New Paganism: Understanding American Culture and the Role of the Church* (New York: Harper & Row, 1987), p. 49.
19. Fox, *Pagans and Christians*, p. 253.

20. Eliade, *A History of Religious Ideas*, Vol. 1, p. 283.
21. Eliade, *A History of Religious Ideas*, Vol. 1, p. 288.
22. Parrinder, *World Religions from Ancient History to the Present*, pp. 157, 158.
23. Seligman, *The History of Magic and the Occult*, p. 48.
24. Eliade, *A History of Religious Ideas*, Vol. 1, p. 260.
25. John Holland Smith, *The Death of Classical Paganism* (New York: Charles Scribner's Sons, 1976), p. 249.
26. Fox, *Pagans and Christians*, p. 160.
27. Daniel 8:5-22.

CHAPTER TEN: *Rome: Christians and Pagans Take Off the Gloves*

1. Davies, *Human Sacrifice*, pp. 50, 51.
2. Harold Lindsell, *The New Paganism: Understanding American Culture and the Role of the Church* (New York: Harper & Row, 1987), p. 14.
3. S. Angus, *The Mystery-Religions* (New York: Dover Publications, 1975), pp.277, 278, 281.
4. Acts 5:1-11.
5. Revelation 2:20-23.
6. Robin Lane Fox, *Pagans and Christians* (New York: Alfred A. Knopf, Inc., 1987), p. 94.
7. Fox, *Pagans and Christians*, p. 261.
8. Fox, *Pagans and Christians*, p. 330.
9. Angus, *The Mystery-Religions*, pp. 277, 278, 281.
10. Angus, *The Mystery-Religions*, p. 272.
11. Acts 2:23, 36.
12. Fox, *Pagans and Christians*, p. 323.
13. Fox, *Pagans and Christians*, p. 324.
14. Fox, *Pagans and Christians*, p. 261.
15. Daniel 2:34, 35, 44, 45.

CHAPTER ELEVEN: *Paganism A.D.*

1. Robin Lane Fox, *Pagans and Christians* (New York: Alfred A. Knopf, Inc., 1987), pp. 404-407.
2. *The New Encyclopedia Britannica*, Vol. 25, p. 95.
3. *The New Encyclopedia Britannica*, Vol. 25, p. 89.
4. *The New Encyclopedia Britannica*, Vol. 25, p. 89.
5. Kurt Seligman,*The History of Magic and the Occult* (New York: Harmony Books, 1975), p. 253.
6. Seligman,*The History of Magic and the Occult*, pp. 286–290.
7. Seligman,*The History of Magic and the Occult*, pp. 294, 295.
8. Seligman,*The History of Magic and the Occult*, p. 311.
9. Seligman,*The History of Magic and the Occult*, p. 311.
10. Nevill Drury,*The Occult Experience: Magic in the New Age* (Garden City Park, NY: Avery Publishing Group, Inc., 1989), pp. 94, 95.
11. Seligman,*The History of Magic and the Occult*, p. 312.
12. Seligman,*The History of Magic and the Occult*, pp. 300-303, under the chapter title "Revolt Against Reason."

13. Seligman, *The History of Magic and the Occult*, pp. 297, 298.
14. Seligman, *The History of Magic and the Occult*, pp. 300-303, under the chapter title "Revolt Against Reason."
15. Arnold Dallimore, *George Whitefield: The Life and Times of the Great Evangelist of the Eighteenth-Century Revival* (Westchester, IL: Crossway Books, 1970), Volume 1, p. 288.

CHAPTER TWELVE: *The Endarkenment Strikes*

1. John Holland Smith, *The Death of Classical Paganism* (New York: Charles Scribner's Sons, 1976), p. 248.
2. Harold Lindsell, *The New Paganism: Understanding American Culture and the Role of the Church* (New York: Harper & Row, 1987), p. 43.
3. Lindsell, *The New Paganism*, pp. 40, 42, 43.
4. Lindsell, *The New Paganism*, p. 42.
5. Lindsell, *The New Paganism*, p. 45.
6. Lindsell, *The New Paganism*, p. 45.
7. Lindsell, *The New Paganism*, p. 45.
8. *Fringes of Reason*, p. 22.
9. *Fringes of Reason*, p. 30.
10. *Fringes of Reason*, p. 27.
11. Nevill Drury, *The Occult Experience: Magic in the New Age* (Garden City Park, NY: Avery Publishing Group, Inc., 1989), p. 45.
12. Numerous good books irrefutably prove this point. Some of the best are:

Samuel Blumenfeld. *Is Public Education Necessary?* Phoenix, AZ: Research Publications.
Samuel Blumenfeld. *NEA: Trojan Horse in American Education.* Phoenix, AZ: Research Publications.
Mel and Norma Gabler with James C. Hefley. *What Are They Teaching Our Children?* Victor Books/Scripture Press.
Richard Mitchell. *The Graves of Academe.* Boston: Little, Brown & Co, 1985.
Barbara Morris. *Change Agents in the Schools.* Carlsbad, CA: Barbara Morris Report, 1984.
Phyllis Schlafly, ed. *Child Abuse in the Classroom.* Westchester, IL: Crossway Books, 1984.
Charles J. Sykes. *Profscam: Professors and the Demise of Higher Education.* Washington, DC: Regnery Gateway, 1988.
Paul Vitz. *Censorship: Evidence of Bias in Our Children's Textbooks.* Ann Arbor, MI: Servant Books, 1986.
Full reviews and ordering information for all these books is in Mary Pride's *New Big Book of Home Learning* (Westchester, IL: Crossway Books, 1988).

13. Lindsell, *The New Paganism*, p. 92.

CHAPTER THIRTEEN: *An End to Evil Empires*

1. Joseph Story, *Commentaries on the Constitution of the United States*, 2nd ed. (Boston: Little, Brown, 1905) 2 vols, 2:593–595.
2. See, for example:

   Verna M. Hall. *The Christian History of the Constitution of the United States of America.* San Francisco: The Foundation for American Christian Education, 1975.
   Tim LaHaye. *Faith of Our Founding Fathers.* Brentwood, TN: Wolgemuth & Hyatt Publishers, 1988.
   John Whitehead. *An America Dream.* Westchester, IL: Crossway Books, 1987.
   John Whitehead. *The Second American Revolution.* Westchester, IL: Crossway Books, 1982.

3. The Rev. Charles H. Dunahoo, coordinator for education and publications of the P.C.A., actually said this in an interview in *Insight* magazine of May 8, 1989, pp. 62, 63. In doing so he was just echoing the tied-to-statistics, anti-revival view of other P.C.A. speakers we have heard. Amazing that anyone who dedicates his life to the advancement of the Christian church doesn't believe it can actually happen.

INDEX